# Brief Lives:
# Johann Wolfgang
# von Goethe

Andrew Piper

ET REMOTISSIMA PROPE

Brief Lives
Published by Hesperus Press Limited
4 Rickett Street, London sw6 1RU
www.hesperuspress.com

First published by Hesperus Press Limited, 2010

Designed and typeset by Fraser Muggeridge studio
Printed in Jordan by Jordan National Press

ISBN: 978-1-84391-910-0

# Contents

*Nature wanted to know how she looked, so she made Goethe.*
Heinrich Heine

# Beginnings

'Living as I do in millennia…' So began one of Goethe's many observations recorded toward the end of his life by his dutiful secretary, Johann Peter Eckermann. It expressed the extraordinary intellectual ambition that surrounded Goethe his entire life and captured the sheer intellectual breadth of a writer who, perhaps more than any other in the entire tradition of Western literature, tried to know more about everything. Religion, literature, politics, history, art, architecture, drama, geology, anatomy, botany, mythology, mining, cartography, optics, even numismatics – Goethe was conversant in all of these fields, informed, up-to-date, and very often a participant in all of the latest breakthroughs. He ran a mine, oversaw a university, discovered a bone in the human skull, collected thousands of rocks, and met Napoleon, all the while writing some of the most elegant, sophisticated, and influential works of literature in history. He participated in the birth of the international bestseller (*The Sorrows of Young Werther*), the rebirth of the novella as a modern form (*Conversations of German Refugees*), the invention of the Bildungsroman (*Wilhelm Meister's Apprenticeship*), produced the archetype of modern man (*Faust*), and through his poetry described the world in more sinuous, luscious detail than ever before. As Heine quipped, Nature did indeed make Goethe so that we could understand her.

If Goethe imaginatively participated in the culture of thousands of years, his actual life coincided with some of the more decisive transformations of European society. During his almost eighty-three years, Goethe lived through the Seven Years' War, the French Revolution, the end of the Holy Roman Empire, the Congress of Vienna, Waterloo and the July Revolution of 1830 in France. He saw the fall of the *Ancien Régime* and the rise of nationalism and the nation state (though the latter not in Germany), a transformation that would generate enormous prosperity in the nineteenth century and the terrible consequences of two world wars in the twentieth. Through all of this Goethe lived as an aloof Privy Counsellor to a minor Duke of a small court in a town of a few thousand inhabitants. He dreamt of Italy and went to the spa. As he once remarked to a friend, 'When people think I'm in Weimar, then I'm already in Erfurt.' His life, like his work, was always about moving on. What makes him so hard to follow (in the sense of to understand and to come after) was precisely the way he saw things so singularly, the way he impressed everything he did with a deeply individual sensibility. This book is an attempt to track that elusive breadth that was uniquely Goethe's.

Johann Wolfgang von Goethe was born in Frankfurt am Main at the stroke of noon on 28th August 1749. As he tells us in his autobiography, fortune played a role right from the start: it was thought to be a stillbirth and only after a great many efforts did the child survive. He was born to Dr Johann Caspar Goethe and Catharina Elisabeth Goethe. The newborn, who was Catharina's first, was named after his maternal grandfather, Johann Wolfgang Textor, who was the Schultheiss (or mayor) of the city of Frankfurt for almost three decades.

The Goethes were a well-off and well-connected family, although not at the very upper echelons of Frankfurt society. Goethe's father, whose own father had arrived in Frankfurt as a tailor, had made his money through trade, and after a failed attempt to enter into city governance he retired from public life at the age of thirty-two. This left him ample time to undertake projects like renovating the family home and organising his children's education, which he participated in with eclectic zeal. Six children came after Goethe, but the only one to survive into adulthood was his sister Cornelia, who was fifteen months younger. Cornelia and Goethe were inseparable as children, and Goethe fondly recounts in his autobiography their numerous escapades together, like the time they secretly memorised a portion of Klopstock's *Messiah* and then surprised their father with a performance while he was being shaved at home by the barber. Not only had their father forbidden this book on the grounds that it wasn't 'poetry' (because it didn't rhyme), he also pointed out that such surprises were rather dangerous, if not outright life-threatening, when the barber had a razor in his hand. Cornelia was Goethe's first and probably truest love, and after her death in childbirth at the age of twenty-six, Goethe would spend the rest of his life searching for and falling in love with sister-figures.

If trolling through his father's personal library of over 1,700 volumes of books was one of the principal aspects of Goethe's early education, his father was the other important pole. Along with a revolving set of part-time tutors (eight in all), Goethe's father coordinated his son's and daughter's education. Religion, Latin, Italian, Yiddish, Hebrew, Greek, drawing, history, geography, handwriting, and music were all studied according to no particular plan. Indeed that was the plan. It was here, through the father's inclination towards all things Italian, that we can see the seeds of Goethe's future love of Italy taking shape. To understand how much his father's participation in his education impacted the young Goethe, we need only recall the story of Goethe's reaction to the death of his younger brother, Hermann Jakob, who died at the age of six. When asked if he had cared for his younger brother, the nine-year-old Goethe reluctantly pulled out from under his bed a stack of papers which he had written on and which he was going to use to teach his younger brother – just like his father had taught him. While Goethe never had very many kind words to say about his father later in life, preferring instead to emphasise his sternness (probably true) or his stinginess (decidedly not true), Goethe's pedagogical interests inherited from his father stayed with him his entire life.

Goethe's mother, on the other hand, was an altogether different matter. Exuberant, warm, boisterous, and odd, she was the spirit who infused Goethe with his deep sense of individuality. She referred to all of Goethe's literary friends who frequented the family home as 'dear son', embraced the Dowager Duchess to everyone's great consternation, apparently wore a plume of feathers to greet the great Madame de Staël, and had a partridge as a pet. She was nature personified and never tired of dispensing useful advice to Goethe such as, 'Stay German, even in your letters!', in reference to attempts by publishers to modernise German typography from gothic to roman letters. As Faust would later say to Mephisto, 'The Mothers! Mothers!... It sounds so exotic.' Nevertheless, Goethe would only visit his mother three times in the thirty years she was alive after he left home and then didn't return to Frankfurt upon her death in 1808. She never received an invitation to come and visit him in Weimar.

The home where Goethe grew up was spacious, with the kitchen on the ground floor and a nook with an open, wooden lattice that looked out onto the street, which Goethe said was his favourite spot in the whole house. It was here that the young boy would throw dishes out the window, much to the amusement of the neighbours. The first floor comprised elegant drawing rooms with large windows that overlooked the street below. Goethe and Cornelia's bedrooms were on the second floor, and Goethe tells us that as he grew older his preferred space in the house was the Garden Room, where he would sit for long hours watching other children play in their real gardens. Goethe's early sense of loneliness, along with his hyper awareness of the contrast between artifice and nature, was incubated in this room. The third floor housed Goethe's study, where he would write until the age of twenty-six when he permanently moved away from home.

The city of Frankfurt (population 36,000) provided the backdrop to Goethe's childhood, and it was a mixture of a cosmopolitan trading centre and an adamantly provincial adherent to municipal custom. It was home to the great trade fairs of Easter and Michaelmas (and the birthplace of the modern book fair), and it supported a good deal of religious diversity, home to sizeable Catholic, Lutheran, and Jewish populations. But as an imperial free city, its governance rested on a complicated and rigid class structure, the town gates were closed every night at half-past eight, and balls were forbidden. It was marked by the narrow, winding streets of an old European medieval city, and the pedestrian was always overshadowed by the fifty-five watchtowers that surrounded the city's perimeter and that guaranteed its independence. Life in Frankfurt was punctuated by the vitality of commercial trade fairs and the rigidity of age-old political ceremonies, like the so-called Court of the Piper. Held once a year on the day before the Birth of Mary (8th September), it was a reenactment of the release from tariffs bequeathed to 'free cities' like Frankfurt by the Emperor. The city leaders (Goethe's grandfather the most senior among them) would convene in the Kaisersaal and there receive symbolic ambassadors accompanied by three pipers bearing a chalice of pepper and a pair of silk gloves. The pepper stood for commercial goods and the gloves for the greeting and blessing of the Emperor. Such local customs were near and dear to every Frankfurter's heart and Goethe never lost this attraction to cultural uniqueness. When he eventually moved to far-off Weimar, Goethe's courtly acquaintances would consistently remark on the pronouncedness of his Frankfurt dialect, which he never lost even into old age.

Goethe was a precocious child, a gifted learner but not a prodigy (like the young Mozart of his day, whom Goethe saw perform as a young boy). He loved to read, had a gift with languages, and soon began writing poems. By the age of nine he said he had read all of Racine and Molière, by the age of twelve he was composing German alexandrines, and shortly after that he began an epistolary novel in six languages. Perhaps not surprisingly, Goethe was less successful among his peers. He tried to join a secret society as a teenager, the 'Arcadian Society of Philandria' or 'League of Virtue', but was rejected. His ability to quote verse at great length was initially seen as entertaining, but his tendency to critique the group's plays was not. 'More chatter than substance,' they said. Goethe's ability to attract and repel others through words was in place right from the start.

And so was his desire to fall in love. At fourteen, Goethe had his first love affair, with a cocktail waitress. This was the first of many to come. But it bore the seeds in many ways of almost all of those future encounters. Not only was she of a lower class than Goethe, it turned out that she was also part of a band of counterfeiters. Goethe being the grandson of the Frankfurt Schultheiss, this was problematic, to say the least. She would eventually leave the city and Goethe. Love, sorrow and a certain illicitness were all mingled together in this first liaison, a constellation that would repeat itself time and again, in both his writing and his life.

# Sentimental Education

Like all young men of his standing, Goethe was shipped off to university at the age of sixteen. He was to study law like his father, not belles-lettres as he wished. Then as now, the question that loomed large was, But what are you going to do with that? Goethe was sent to Leipzig, which was known as 'little Paris' and home to a world-class university. Here there were broad avenues for strolling, not the twisted streets of his hometown, large squares and gardens for seeing and being seen, famous book-shops and publishing houses, fashionable clothes, and renowned professors like Christian Fürchtegott Gellert and Johann Christoph Gottsched. The spirit of the French Rococo was in the air and Goethe quickly updated his wardrobe and tried to hide his accent. Like most well-off students through the ages, Goethe was more interested in life than lectures. He learned to drink beer, attend parties, go to the theatre, gossip about fellow students and marvel at his professors – their ideas, their freedom, and their nineteen-year-old wives.

One of the key influences of Goethe's time in Leipzig was the painter Adam Oeser, who held drawing lessons in his attic and who instilled in Goethe a love of antiquity. It was a time when Johann Joachim Winckelmann's ideas were the rage, put forth in works like *Thoughts on the Imitation of Greek Works in Painting and Sculpture* (1755), in which he wrote, 'The only way for us to become great, perhaps inimitable, is by imitating the ancients.'

Goethe and Oeser would sit together for hours and pore over reproductions of classical art that had been reproduced in Daniel Philipp Lippert's *Dactyliothecae Universalis* (1755). Goethe's interest in drawing would not be some passing college fancy, however, but would become central to his overall artistic development. By the end of his life, he had amassed close to two thousand sheets of his own drawings and possessed a collection of another nine thousand prints of works by various artists. As he would later remark, 'Word and image are correlates that eternally search for one another.'

If Oeser was at work training Goethe's eye during this period, it was a local court tutor, Ernst Wolfgang Behrisch, who trained him to be disdainful. Referred to by university friends as 'the proud dreamer', Goethe refined his sense of being an outcast through his friendship with Behrisch, eleven years his senior. 'We laugh at the Leipzigers,' wrote Goethe to his sister Cornelia about his companionship with Behrisch. Behrisch loathed the world of the book trade and taught Goethe how to feel a certain antipathy to 'the public', feelings that dated back, he tells us in his autobiography, to the extreme partisanship of the Seven Years' War when Goethe was a boy. Goethe never truly relinquished such feelings and it would be several decades before he thought seriously about the world of print and publishing. But then, in typical fashion, he did so in an unprecedentedly sophisticated way.

Goethe's great love of this period was Anna Katharina (Kätchen) Schönkopf, daughter of a local wine merchant, and to her was dedicated the small book of poems, *Annette*, which Behrisch convinced Goethe not to publish but to produce as a bound, illustrated manuscript volume. They were very much of their age, in the spirit of Anacreon, the Greek lyric poet famous for his drinking songs, full of wit, irony, and light erotic touches. In a dramatic gesture in October 1767, Goethe consigned everything he had written before the *Annette* poems to flames. The coming year was a tumultuous one in Goethe's life,

Behrisch having left and his relationship to Kätchen having come undone. Marriage was out of the question (again for class reasons) and so things ended by April. In July, Goethe suffered a haemorrhage and began coughing up blood. By late August he was forced to return home to Frankfurt on his nineteenth birthday, his degree incomplete and his health in great danger.

It was not until that winter that his health began to stabilise and his convalescence was well under way. And as is so often the case, illness provided the occasion for personal transformation. Goethe finally decided that he would dedicate his life to writing. During his time in Frankfurt he came into contact with Fräulein von Klettenberg and her circle and was exposed to the ideas of pietism. Pietism was one of numerous Protestant sects that were cropping up across Europe and North America in the eighteenth century and was based around the principle of recorded introspection. It would be extremely important for a host of eighteenth-century German writers and was part of the surging fascination with the genre of autobiography and the practice of life writing. Goethe's own autobiography, which comprised eleven volumes of his final collected edition, owed much to the pietist tradition, and Klettenberg would one day become the model for the famed character of 'The Beautiful Soul' in Goethe's novel, *Wilhelm Meister's Apprenticeship*.

Frankfurt began to grate on Goethe, as hometowns so often do. He was sent to Strasbourg in the autumn of 1770 to complete his dissertation and here he met Johann Gottfried Herder, who would become one of a handful of the most important influences in Goethe's life. 'Goethe is a good, honourable young man,' wrote Herder to his fiancée, 'with much feeling and at times too much feeling.' Herder was born in the small town of Mohrung in East Prussia and had studied theology in Königsberg (now Kaliningrad), often visiting the lectures of the famed philosopher Immanuel Kant. Herder was an extremely charismatic figure, a born preacher everyone said, who was also a prolific and spirited writer. When Herder arrived in Strasbourg shortly after Goethe, he was not only Goethe's senior by five years. His life as a writer and a leading intellect in the German-speaking territories was well under way. Goethe was still very much learning about his own inclinations as a writer, his concerns, his priorities, and his style. Herder stepped in at that moment to help the young Goethe find his voice.

By the time Herder arrived in Strasbourg, he had already published two works of literary criticism, *On Recent German Literature* and *Critical Forests*. During the year that he and Goethe were in Strasbourg together, Herder would compose his *Treatise on the Origin of Language*, which Goethe would read while Herder was writing and which would eventually win the Royal Academy of Berlin's essay prize, earning him European notoriety. Herder's principal concern was with the renewal of a national language, indeed with the interweaving of these two categories of nation and language together. 'Every nation speaks,' wrote Herder, 'according to how it thinks, and thinks according to how it speaks.' Language was what shaped nations, and poets were the ones who shaped language. 'Poetry is the mother-tongue of man,' Herder tells us. What more did a young poet need to hear?

For Herder, poetry was not a bunch of abstract (and often ancient) rules, but grew out of every nation's soil, *'eine Kultur des Bodens'* (a culture of the ground), as Herder called it. Instead of a system of timeless and universal artistic conventions, Herder's work, more than that of any other theorist of his age, ushered in an era of cultural plurality. 'Every nation bears in itself the standard of its own perfection.' And the same could be said for the poet. Herder's system, which was decidedly unsystematic, rested on the fundamental individuality of the poet, that his writing must emerge from his own nature.

Goethe and Herder would put theory into practice during the first of half of 1771 when they rode out together into the Alsatian countryside recording and collecting local ballads and folksongs. Such work, which eventually made its way into Herder's collection of folksongs from across Europe, proved to be enormously influential for a later generation of Romantic writers like Walter Scott, who himself would one day journey by horseback into the countryside of the Scottish border with his friend John Leyden and collect ballads for his famed collection, *Minstrelsy of the Scottish Border* (1802–3). Herder's canon of Homer, Shakespeare, Ossian, and the Icelandic *Edda* comprised Goethe's reading from this period and would later make up the core of the Romantic canon along with Spanish Golden Age writers like Cervantes and medieval Germanic epics like the *Nibelungenlied*. The 'literary despotism', as Ludwig Tieck called it, of French classical theatre was gradually coming to a close.

During these heady days with Herder, Goethe was also at work on more mundane matters like completing his dissertation, a study of the secular origins of ecclesiastical law. It was rejected by the faculty in Leipzig as too controversial – and perhaps too unsystematic. Either way, Goethe was offered the option of acquiring the alternative title, '*Licentiatus Juris*', by engaging in a series of public legal debates, according to custom. Goethe's theses for the debates oscillated between the traditional and the outlandish and the event bordered on the farcical. But he passed and was granted the right to practise law.

The other great influence of this period in Goethe's life was once again a love affair, this time with Friederike Brion, a pastor's daughter who lived in the nearby village of Sesenheim. Goethe visited frequently and later in the spring even spent a few weeks with the Brions. There were picnics and dances and Goethe entertained the family with stories and the recitation of poetry. During the spring he wrote his collection of poems, *Songs of Sesenheim*, with opening lines like, 'Oh, I long for you' and 'My heart pounded, quick let's ride'. He tells us his favourite book from this period was Goldsmith's *The Vicar of Wakefield*, a classic sentimental novel about village family life. It was an indication of just how much Goethe was attached to the idea of domesticity. As Werther proclaimed while reading his Homer, 'In the mornings, I go out at sunrise to my Walheim to pick sugar peas in the innkeeper's garden and sit down and peel them while reading my Homer. Then I choose a pot from the small kitchen, scoop out some butter, put the peas on the fire and cover them… Nothing fills me with such a true and restful feeling as the habits of patriarchal life.' But it was, for Goethe, never more than an idea. As time passed, so too did Goethe's amorous fervour. By August he would pay a final visit, leaving Friederike and Strasbourg behind.

Goethe's breakup with Friederike was not without consequence in his life. It was clear that they had spent a great deal of time together, much of it alone. What this entailed, no one knows for certain, despite ample speculation on the matter. What we do know is that it would have been understood that such behaviour implied at least an unofficial engagement. Goethe's departure marked an enormous breach of custom and an insult to the family. As he wrote in his autobiography, 'Here for the first time I was guilty.' When he returned home to Frankfurt to practise law, he arrived in time for the scandalous trial of Susanna Margaretha Brandt, who was accused of killing her illegitimate child and who would later provide the model for the heroine, Gretchen, in Goethe's *Faust*. It was a visceral reminder of his own potential negligence. In six intense weeks during the fall of 1771 while the trial unfolded before him, Goethe wrote the historical drama, *Götz von Berlichingen with the Iron Hand*, which would bring him his early fame. Writing, then and throughout his life, was a cure for the inevitable coupling of desire and guilt that Goethe saw at the heart of human affairs. Brandt was publicly executed on 14th January 1772.

# Early Fame

After returning to Frankfurt, Goethe began to practise law. As with all of his subsequent administrative duties, it was a lacklustre performance. He handled twenty-eight cases in four years and was reprimanded by the court for his inflammatory rhetoric in the briefs he submitted. But it was also a period of intense creative output that resulted in the emergence of a star on the stage of European literature.

Goethe's *Götz* became the founding document of the movement known as '*Sturm und Drang*' or 'Storm and Stress'. With its turn towards the old Germanic culture of chivalric knights, *Götz* embodied an emerging historical consciousness that owed much to Herder's thinking. A nation's past was coming to be seen as key to understanding its identity and future. As Goethe wrote in his paean to the immense, Gothic cathedral of Strasbourg during this same period, 'This is German architecture, *our* architecture.' The past was an integral part of the story of a nation's cultural 'development'. Nation and man became mirror images of one another, each with their own childhoods, adolescences and stages of full-blown maturity. The subsequent rage for historical novels such as Walter Scott's *Ivanhoe* (1820) owed much to this earlier moment. It was no coincidence that Scott was one of the first to translate *Götz* into English.

If *Götz* captured a new sense of national history that was beginning to spread across Europe, it also embodied an emerging spirit of cultural defiance. With its over fifty places of action and its virtual unstageability, Goethe's drama defied the rules of French classical theatre, taking instead the English Shakespeare as its avowed model. It rejected poetic norms in favour of a 'natural' poetics. The poet was now a 'genius', beholden not to rules but to his own nature. As Gottfried August Bürger, author of one of the most famous ballads in the German language and a key figure of the Storm and Stress movement, wrote to his friend, Heinrich Boie, 'Boie! Boie! The knight with the iron hand, what a play! I can't control myself from sheer enthusiasm. How can I reveal my delight to the author? One could indeed call him the German Shakespeare… Free! Free! Subject to no one but nature!'

Such cultural defiance often bordered on the political. Götz captured a growing desire for heroic individualism, for a return to the age of *Faustrecht*, or the law of the fist, that embodied a sense of self unfettered by the rules of society or religion. As Goethe would write – addressing the god Zeus at the close of one his most famous early poems, 'Prometheus' – about the titan who had stolen the gods' fire:

> Here I sit, forming men
> After my own image
> A race equal to me,
> to suffer, weep,
> Savour and enjoy,
> And scorn you,
> Like me!

Nothing was a more palpable rejection of the long tradition of the divine origins of poetry – from Homer to Dante to Milton to Goethe's own immediate antecedent, Klopstock – than Prometheus' opening challenge, 'Cover your heaven, Zeus.' And nothing captured the anti-authoritarian spirit of the age more than that brazen command directed at the highest authority of all. Here the seeds of Goethe's *Faust* were being planted and it was during this period that he would make his first forays into working on this quintessential Germanic myth.

The fist and the iron hand were crucial symbols for expressing a larger sense of social dissatisfaction during the 1770s in the German states, one that was quickly spreading across Europe. But they also represented only one half of the equation that such emotional outpouring could embody. Alongside this band of angry young men, there also raged the cult of sentimentality. More than ever before or since, people cried, whether in novels or in their letters about novels.

Goethe was introduced into this world during his time in Frankfurt in the nearby city of Darmstadt through his friend and colleague, Johann Heinrich Merck, who had begun editing the weekly review, *The Frankfurt Literary Advertiser*, to which Goethe had become a contributor. Darmstadt was a small city, seventeen miles from Frankfurt and home to a fallen court where the princesses wore cotton and the prince collected toy soldiers. There Goethe met the group called 'The Community of Saints', led by the court tutor, Franz Michael Leuchsenring. Klopstock was their professed idol, the 'ode' the popular new genre, and 'pindaric' the adjective of the day (it meant 'free-flowing'). The women were all given nicknames after Greek goddesses or flowers, like Psyche (Caroline Flachsland), Urania (Henriette von Roussillon), or Lila (Luise von Ziegler). When Goethe walked the seventeen miles between Frankfurt and Darmstadt on a wet, wintry day in 1772, he was given the name 'The Wanderer'.

The group was held together by a culture of incessant letter-writing, the letters composed with numerous exclamation points and lots of dashes. 'One has no idea how much people write today,' the fictional character Wilhelm would write to his wife in Goethe's later novel, *Wilhelm Meister's Travels*. 'I'm not even talking about what is printed, although that is still plenty. One can only imagine how much is circulated in silence through letters about the news, stories, reports, anecdotes and descriptions of people's lives today.' As Wilhelm noted, and as Goethe would repeatedly reflect, it seemed as if everyone towards the closing decades of the eighteenth century was writing – not only a great deal, but also interminably about their own feelings. The improved postal system of the House of Thurn and Taxis had much to do with this new confessional epistolary culture, but so did English novels like Richardson's *Pamela* and French novels like Rousseau's *Julie*. Writing and feeling were increasingly imagined to be synonymous and simultaneous. As Faust, the herald of the new age, would proclaim, 'Feeling is everything.'

An important complement to the sentimental community in Darmstadt was the group known as the 'Göttinger Grove'. Its members included Heinrich Boie, the editor of the annual poetry anthology, *Almanach of the Muses*, where some of Goethe's early poetry would appear, and Johann Heinrich Voß, who would become the famed translator of Homer. The group acquired its name when the participants pledged their allegiance to the cause of poetry during a moonlit night one evening in the woods outside of Göttingen. Such groups began sprouting up all over the German territories and Goethe would capture this spirit of rampant, poetic sentimentality in his poem 'Ganymede', about the young boy abducted by Zeus, who lives and loves among the gods:

*The clouds waft*
*Down, the clouds*
*Tend toward the yearning love,*
*Toward me, me!*
*In your lap*
*Upwards!*
*Embracing embraced!*
*Upwards towards your breast,*
*All-loving Father!*

In those repeated exclamation points and the circularity enacted in the words 'embracing embraced', one could see the effusions of sentimental culture at work. But in that double 'me' ('Toward me, me!') one also intuited the fundamental solipsism that was at the heart of eighteenth-century sentimentality, an almost perfect complement to the radical individualism of the Storm and Stress (as in Prometheus' defiant, 'Like me!'). The self and its feelings had become the ultimate measure of all things, but how was one to sustain any sense of commonality in a world of the divine 'me'? It was from this brew of solipsism, epistolary culture, and poetic sentimentality that one of Goethe's most successful writing projects of his entire career, *The Sorrows of Young Werther*, would soon emerge.

In May of 1772, still in his early twenties, Goethe was sent to Wetzlar, home of the Imperial Cameral Court of the Holy Roman Empire, where his grandfather had been sent before him. It was part of Goethe's legal training, but the main reason for going to Wetzlar was not to work – few there seemed to be doing much of it at all – but to meet the rising class of state officials who would one day return to their respective prin-cipalities. Goethe didn't even do much of that. What he did do was fall in love again, this time with Charlotte Buff, the 'Lotte' of Goethe's *Werther*. In June he met her at a ball, an eighteen-year-old daughter of a local bailiff. He spent every Saturday afternoon after dinner with her and her family, and like the fictional Lotte, the real version was also surrounded by eleven younger brothers and sisters. Once again, Goethe immersed himself in a domestic scene that he was not wholly a part of. Charlotte was engaged to Johann Christian Kestner, whom Goethe had befriended prior to meeting her. Kestner gradually grew concerned about Goethe's continued presence, there was a scene, and Charlotte became colder towards the constant guest. By September Goethe had silently departed from yet another domestic world. When Charlotte received Goethe's letter announcing that he had left, Kestner records in his diary that 'tears came into her eyes as she read.' Back in Frankfurt, Goethe hung Charlotte's silhouette on the wall over his bed.

That autumn another key event transpired that would make its way into Goethe's fiction. Karl Wilhelm Jerusalem, whom Goethe had met while in Wetzlar, committed suicide because he was in love with the wife of a friend. Jerusalem's story of impossible love soon made him a cause célèbre in sentimental circles. During the whole next year, Goethe lived in his family home in Frankfurt, and his personal loneliness was contrasted with three marriages of close friends that all took place in that same year: his sister Cornelia to Johann Georg Schlosser, Charlotte Buff to Kestner, and Caroline Flachsland to Goethe's friend Herder. As Goethe said to Sophie von La Roche, 'I am alone, alone, and more so everyday.' Then, in four weeks in February of 1774, Goethe wrote *The Sorrows of Young Werther*. He was for a time the most famous writer in Europe.

# Sorrows, Real and Imagined

*The Sorrows of Young Werther* appeared on the German book market in the autumn of 1774. It is the story of a young man with too much emotion. He falls in love with another man's fiancée, is an incessant reader, and imagines that he can see the entire universe in a blade of grass. By the end of the novel, he will shoot himself in the head as a copy of Lessing's play, *Emilia Galotti*, lies open on his desk.

The novel is composed of letters by Werther addressed to his friend, Wilhelm, who will become the hero of Goethe's next novel. But we never hear his friend's replies as Goethe transforms the popular genre of the epistolary novel into a diary. The letter without a reply is Goethe's way of showing Werther as the consummate outsider. He is spurned by society, a self-described 'pilgrim'. Like Odysseus, his idol, he is a wanderer always in search of a home. His object is to find love, pure love, which he finds in the figure of Lotte, the sister who cares for her siblings:

Climbing the steps I opened the door and beheld the most charming scene I have ever set eyes on. In the hallway, six children between eleven and two were milling about a beautiful young woman of medium height, wearing a simple white dress with pink ribbons on the sleeves and breast. She was holding a loaf of dark bread and cutting a piece for each of the little ones about her, according to their age and appetite.

The sister appears as a mother here, recreating Christianity's virgin mother in a secular, domestic chord (nicely amplified in the Eucharistic gesture of breaking bread with the children). 'Is not my love for her,' Werther will later plaintively ask, 'the most sacred, purest and most brotherly love?' Werther, like Goethe, was always in search of a sister.

The point of *Werther* was to show how literature could teach readers how to feel, and feeling, not courtly artifice, was to be the basis of a new middle class society. Lotte was the embodiment of nature, and nature was to be the foundation of art predicated on feeling. 'Only nature has inexhaustible riches, and only nature creates a great artist,' writes Werther. With its endless dashes, its abrupt turns, its accumulation of digressions, *The Sorrows of Young Werther* was shaped by a writer trying to write to the moment, to imagine how writing could capture one's immediate feelings. But if writing could indeed capture the ebullient feelings of the emotional young man, those feelings always exceeded the world around him. Like Don Quixote before him, Werther was both lovable and a fool.

What made Goethe's *Werther* ultimately so successful was the way it captured the spirit of a generation – it subtly critiqued the excesses of individuality at its core *and* the world's incapacity to accommodate this greater yearning for sympathy and sentiment. Like *Don Quixote*, it left readers wondering whether maybe the hero wasn't a madman after all, maybe we readers had failed to live up to his ideals. As Goethe would remark several decades later to his secretary Eckermann:

The much-discussed age of Werther does not belong, upon closer inspection, to the progression of world culture, but to the progress of every individual, who with a born natural sensibility finds himself inhibited by the ways of an antiquated world. Happiness deterred, productivity blocked, desires unsatisfied – these are not the crimes of a particular age, but of every individual person, and it would indeed be terrible if everyone did not have a phase at least once in his life in which it seemed as though Werther was written just for him.

*The Sorrows of Young Werther* achieved unparalleled success. It was translated into numerous languages, adapted to the stage, parodied, pirated, continued, and discussed in hundreds of subsequent publications. There were Werther porcelain sets, poems about Lotte's feelings on Werther's death, Dantean continuations such as *Werther in Hell*, and playful rejoinders like *The Joys of Young Werther* (the rash of suicides that were said to follow the novel, however, have turned out to be a myth). But most of all, there was enthusiasm and more feeling. 'Werther! Werther! Werther! Oh, what a little book! No other novel has so touched my heart. Goethe is too good, how gladly I would have liked to embrace him while reading!' wrote one reader. 'I read it in a single breath,' wrote another. Written in an outburst of creativity, *Werther* was read with a similar feverish intensity, contributing to an almost endless number of subsequent outbursts by readers.

And of course critique. Werther's suicide was scandalous for eighteenth-century readers, but perhaps not scandalous in the way we might think. After all, heroes of classical theatre had been offing themselves for quite some time. What was new, or at least what posed a certain friction for critics, was the way the novel provided so little pedagogical guidance vis-à-vis the main character. Was Werther a noble figure or a fool? It was so hard to tell. He said so many moving things and yet acted in such unattractive ways. The editor who emerged towards the end of the novel and who might have held out the promise of framing a critical position in fact withheld judgment with delightful precision. Like Werther's free style, the reader was left to his or her own interpretive freedom. That is what made the novel such a problem. As one reviewer from the United States put it, 'It is a book more read than any of its kind by the young, and which has proved the bane of more than one family.'

Goethe was now the 'author of Werther' and would remain so until he became the 'author of Faust' some three decades later. He was famous, but in a way that did not entirely satisfy him. He was popular, but also misunderstood. His book was loved and despised for equally wrong reasons. He regretted having written the book for his whole life. 'Since it appeared I have only read it once and have protected myself from doing so again.'

If an authorial future had begun to open itself up to Goethe by the end of 1774, so too had a social one. The future Duke of Saxe-Weimar, Carl August, was about to turn eighteen and was sent on a tour in December in search of a wife. His brother's tutor, Karl Ludwig von Knebel, could not resist a visit to the author of *Werther* along the way. The young author impressed him, with not just his literary learning, but also his knowledge of the world. Goethe was later introduced to the Duke in Mainz, and for a few days they ice-skated and passed the time talking of life and literature. One member of the entourage was Baron von Stein, whose wife, Charlotte, wrote to inquire about the potential new addition to the Weimar circle. The philosopher, Johann Georg Zimmermann, wrote back to her with the foreboding words, 'You do not realise how dangerous this lovable and enchanting man could be for you.' She would soon become one of the most important loves of Goethe's life.

When Goethe returned to Frankfurt, he learned that Fräulein von Klettenberg had died while he was away. The guilt of un-attended death would be a constant in Goethe's life, but so would his subsequent memorialisation of loved ones through his writing. And as was so often the case, Goethe would replace one beautiful soul for another in short order. Goethe soon began a letter correspondence with an anonymous admirer of *Werther* whom he had never met, but whom he later learned was the Countess Augusta von Stolberg. Such distant love was then

28

complemented by a new affair, this time with Lili Schönemann, daughter of a prominent Frankfurt banking family. Goethe fell in love in a deeper way than he ever had in his life. They were engaged, exchanging two gold hearts with one another. As Goethe told his confidant Eckermann towards the final years of life, 'She was indeed the first whom I deeply and truly loved. And I can also say she was the last.'

Lili was an intelligent, witty, and beautiful young woman, a perfect equal for Goethe's spirit. She was also the first woman in Goethe's life who neither was already engaged nor posed problems of social class. She was marriageable. With her, Goethe would become a lawyer and live in Frankfurt. Goethe plainly saw his future – and balked. It would be another three decades until he finally married. His poetry, his sense of self, the intimate relationship between unquenched desire and profound creativity that he saw at the heart of his writing – these would all vanish were he to become domesticated, or so he feared. Unlike his traumatic separation from Friederike, however, Goethe was careful to leave his affair with Lili unconsummated and thus leave Lili's social status untainted.

In the spring of 1775, Goethe began to socialise with Augusta von Stolberg's brothers and headed to Switzerland on an eighteenth-century version of the road trip. It was an escape from the pressures of domestic life and also just something to do. They drank lots of wine, threw glasses, and dressed up as Werther. They visited Johann Caspar Lavater in Zurich, author of the *Physiognomic Fragments*, and went to the lake where Klopstock had written one of his most famous odes. Goethe, too, brought a notebook, and along the shore under the hanging trees he wrote one of his greatest poems, 'On the Lake', which concludes with the lines:

*Twinkling on the surface*
*Thousands of swaying stars,*
*Drinking lovely mist*

*Round the spires afar,*
*A morning breeze besets*
*Upon the shaded inlet*
*And now the lake reflects*
*The ripening fruit.*

In this poem we can see Goethe beginning to move away from the principles that had guided him during his early period. The immediacy of a poem like 'The Song of May' ('How superbly nature/ Illuminates *me*') or the solipsism of 'Ganymede' ('The clouds waft/ Down… Towards *me, me!*') is superseded here by an interaction with nature and an artistry of reflection. Nature's illumination is now *refracted* in those broken points of celestial light scattered across the wavy surface of the lake. Its presence is similarly consumed by the drinking mist or encircling breeze. Insight is fleeting here. 'On the Lake' insists on the centrality of the singular, meaningful moment as the ripening fruit is dynamically fixed on the undulating surface of the water. Time is momentarily arrested, but in its stoppage we feel the impress of its potential flow, that it cannot be held back for long, like those heavy, dangling fruits.

After the tour concluded, during which Goethe also produced a great number of drawings showing once more how integrally related his writing was to seeing, Goethe returned to Frankfurt – and Lili – for the summer. Both of them knew the relationship was coming to a close, but neither was capable of letting it end. Goethe tells us he was 'drifting', as the natural landscape of the lake serves as the point of reference for making sense of this unhappy time in his life. Afraid to marry, with little investment in his own career, and uninterested in living at home anymore, he was directionless. It was a youthful moment probably familiar to most, when a stage of life has passed but what comes next is not yet clear. Several decades later it will all make sense, but right then in that moment, the claustrophobia and the drift can feel immense.

But there was still a sense of optimism, as in youth there so often is. As Goethe would write to Augusta von Stolberg:

What a life. Should I continue on? or end it for eternity? And yet, dear, when I feel again that in the middle of all this nothingness so many layers are shed from my heart, so that the convulsive stress of my little foolish composition dissipates, my view of the world becomes more jovial, my interactions with others more certain, regular, and extensive. And yet at the same time my mind remains dedicated to an eternal, sacred love... Then I can continue on.

Even in stasis there was a sense that Goethe was still developing, indeed stasis was the necessary component of development. Towards the end of the summer Goethe sent a letter to Knebel inquiring about life in Weimar. In September, the Duke offered an invitation to come to court. Carl August visited Frankfurt again to press his case. Goethe's father was wary of the fate of a middle-class *Bürger* at a princely court. The Duke was said to admire greatly the slightly older writer. 'I enjoy his company a great deal because he is so natural,' the Duke said. A formal invitation followed in October, but no one showed up to bring Goethe to Weimar. Father and son grew impatient, a tour of Italy was planned. 'I packed for the North and am travelling to the South,' Goethe said. Once again there was a sense of purposelessness.

It turned out that Goethe's travelling companion had been delayed. The luminaries in Weimar were anxiously awaiting Goethe's arrival. Goethe was met by carriage in Heidelberg and turned around. He arrived in Weimar on 7th November 1775. He could finally indulge in Werther's sentiment, with which his renowned novel had begun: 'How happy I am to be away!'

# Weimar, Capital of the Eighteenth Century

Weimar was a small town of six thousand inhabitants, no larger than a suburb of Goethe's hometown of Frankfurt. The roads were terrible and no post road even came into Weimar. The ducal palace had burned down the year before Goethe arrived and the newly married rulers lived in temporary housing. Like many European principalities, Weimar in the eighteenth century was a world of stark contrasts, poor peasants providing the livelihood of a small coterie of aristocrats. Little middle-class commercial trade existed in Weimar and the neighbouring regions. What little there was largely existed to serve the court.

If Weimar itself was smaller than Goethe's Frankfurt, the world over which it wielded power was considerably larger, close to a hundred thousand citizens. However small and fractured, principalities like Saxe-Weimar-Eisenach, as it was officially called, were the major power centres in the complex eighteenth-century world of German politics. It would remain so until Germany was unified under Prussian absolutist rule in the late nineteenth century. For a writer like Goethe to go to Weimar was part of a natural trend in eighteenth-century German intellectual life. It would be many years before it was possible to make a living from one's pen, so that going to a court was simply a strategic move to find a patron. Klopstock, Wieland, and Lessing had all done the same. At the same time, accompanying a duke or prince at court was also a perceived way of wielding power, certainly far more than could ever be exercised in an urban setting such as Frankfurt. There was a pedagogical spirit in the air that fostered hope for educating enlightened monarchs to take German society into the next century. But ever since Plato went to Syracuse, philosophy and art's proximity to power has been a fraught experience, to say the least. The story of Goethe in Weimar is yet another cautionary tale about what happens when the prince of poets gets too close to the prince.

Court life in Weimar was extremely formal. Dinner, cards and concerts were hosted a few nights every week, and attendees were required to follow a strict dress code of elegant silk garments. Goethe was not allowed to eat at the Duke's table until he was named a Privy Counsellor and even then he was not allowed to participate in evening soirées until he had been ennobled. In the summers, high society would retreat to their various summer estates, retiring from the strict schedule of courtly social life.

If Weimar was on the one hand nothing more than a traditional, old-fashioned, and stodgy world of cliquish courtiers (referred to as a 'murderous nest' by one outsider), it was also fast gaining a reputation for being an intellectual centre. Under the direction of the Duke's mother, Anna Amalia, who had run the Duchy until Carl August turned eighteen, Weimar had come to be known as the 'court of the muses'. Anna Amalia had grown up in nearby Brunswick with its legendary ducal library in Wolfenbüttel (still preserved today), had an interest in reading the classics and was versed in a well-rounded arts education. When she appointed Christoph Martin Wieland, who was a professor of philosophy in Erfurt and one of the German language's most renowned living writers, to be Carl August's tutor in 1772, she was rejecting the traditional training of the aristocracy into the world of power politics in exchange for the cultivation, so she hoped, of a more enlightened ruler. When Wieland began publishing his popular journal, the *Teutsche Merkur*, which was modelled on the *Mercure de France*, Weimar emerged as an important hub of German, and later European, letters. It would mark the beginning of a continuous circulation over the next several decades of some of Germany's most important thinkers through this small capital and its neighbouring university town of Jena, later the birthplace of German Romanticism. How this village came to represent such an intellectual centre – so that it could later become the symbolic capital of Germany's first experiment with democracy in the twentieth century – is a complex story of intellectual networking, fame and the singular place that Goethe came to occupy within the world of European arts and letters.

But the days of radiance were still a long way off. The opening months of Goethe's stay in Weimar were, simply put, wild ones. One has to imagine an eighteen-year-old absolute monarch with a 25-year-old poet as his mentor to get a sense of the state of things. There were sleigh rides, parties at the hunting lodge, ice skating, drinking and more drinking, adolescent pranks, and many, many dalliances with the local peasant girls. 'Things are terrifying there,' wrote one observer. 'The Duke runs loose with Goethe around the local villages like a crazy student. He gets drunk, and shares girls with him in a brotherly manner. A minister who tried to dissuade him from these pranks because of his health was told that he needed to do them in order to strengthen himself!' One infamous evening, the Duke and Goethe rode out together and exchanged clothing before they met up with some local women.

Needless to say, Goethe's arrival was not always welcome. By the end of that first summer, he was forced to ask some of his younger companions to leave town. But he maintained his support through a few key alliances. Not only was the Duke an enormous supporter of Goethe, but so was the Duke's mother. At thirty-five, she still played an active role in court life, holding important gatherings at the Wittumspalais where she resided. She saw in Goethe an important counterweight to the schemers at court and hoped he might yet help her son live up to her ideals of the educated, enlightened ruler. Goethe was not just an aide-de-camp for Carl August's amorous outings, he also introduced a theatrical, cultural element to everyday life in Weimar. Impromptu plays in the woods, lavish annual birthday celebrations for Carl August's wife, the Duchess Luise, poetry readings – over all these events Goethe presided like an impresario.

Wieland, too, played a key role in vouching for Goethe's character. As the Duke's former tutor and the first luminary of the court of the muses, his word was worth something. Even as someone who had initially been the object of Goethe's sharp tongue (in Goethe's parody *Gods, Heroes and Wieland*), Wieland had come to feel great affection for the younger writer after meeting him. 'Since this morning,' Wieland wrote to a friend after their initial contact, 'my soul is full of Goethe, like a drop of dew before the morning sun.' Wieland's feelings for Goethe were a sign of just how powerfully Goethe could impress another writer. However much Goethe could at times alienate people he met with his erratic behaviour ('One needs a certain fortitude of the soul to remain his friend,' said one acquaintance), it was clear that to someone who loved language and literature Goethe was an inspiration.

Things gradually quietened down and Goethe soon settled into his new administrative life. He was appointed Privy Counsellor on 11th June 1776. Although the Prime Minister threatened to resign upon hearing the news, Goethe was soon integrated into bureaucratic dealings, meeting regularly with the Duke and the two other members of his council to discuss the affairs of government – taxes, foreign relations, and the business of local mines, roads, and military recruitment. For the next decade in his role as Privy Counsellor, Goethe was busy. He was appointed head of the War Commission, the Highways Commission, the Mines Commission, and was eventually named Chancellor of the Exchequer. He led an initiative to reopen a silver mine in nearby Ilmenau, which eventually turned out to be a financial disaster. On the other hand, when the duchy was on the verge of a major financial crisis in 1782, Goethe stepped in to rectify the government's finances and avoid defaulting on its debt by convincing the Duke to cut his military expenditures drastically. Over time, however, it dawned on Goethe that administrative life absorbed too much of his time and energy and its impact seemed too marginal for the effort. By the mid 1780s, before he secretly departed for Italy, Goethe had effectively given up on governance. As he would say to a friend, 'Anyone who meddles in administration must either be a philistine, a knave or a fool.'

During this period in Goethe's life, he was living in the Duke's two-storey garden house, located in an idyllic spot in the park overlooking the Ilm river and the ducal residence. Here Goethe could leave behind the intrigues of court and tend to his garden. He would hold Easter-egg hunts every spring (no parents were allowed) and reward the children with gifts like old-German chapbooks. Goethe loved children, and he would eventually become the tutor to Fritz, the youngest child of Charlotte von Stein, often allowing him to spend the night. As Goethe would write in *Werther*, 'Yes, my dear Wilhelm, nothing on earth is closer to my heart than children.'

It was here in the garden house that Goethe would watch the mist rise in the morning and the moon rise at night, looking for the repose that he desperately sought but seldom found. It was here that he would write poems like 'The Wanderer's Night Song', with the words:

*What is the use of all this pain and desire?*
*Sweet peace,*
*Come, oh come into my breast!*

Goethe's writing did not stop during his initial administrative immersion in Weimar, but it did change. It was marked by an aspect of incompletion, as the days of writing entire works in four weeks were over. His play *Iphigenia in Tauris* had not yet been turned into verse, *Egmont* remained incomplete, *Torquato Tasso* was only as far as the second act, *Faust* received little attention, and his novel, *Wilhelm Meister's Theatrical Mission*, which later became the basis of *Wilhelm Meister's Apprenticeship*, was underway but far from done. The dramatic works all concerned a hero who struggled to survive within a courtly world. Iphigenia was held captive by the barbarian Thoas, Tasso by a foreign prince on the grounds that he, Tasso, was insane. *Wilhelm Meister* was about a young man who wanted to be an artist, not a businessman or a courtier. Goethe's works from this period provide a poignant image of how hard it was for him to be a writer at court.

If it was a period of incompletion, it was also one of incubation. Much of what came to be known as Goethe's classical corpus was already underway. The plays, when coupled with the work of the great dramatist Friedrich Schiller, who would arrive in Weimar a decade later, would become some of the most influential dramatic works of German literary history. *Wilhelm Meister*, in its revised form, would initiate an entirely new genre and provide a key reference point for a subsequent generation of German Romantic writers.

But for now, it was a season of change, and much was changing around Goethe as well. Kant would publish his epoch-making *Critique of Pure Reason* in 1781, Herder would begin his *Ideas for a Philosophy of History* in 1784, Karl Philipp Moritz gave the novel a new autobiographical dimension with *Anton Reiser* in 1785, and Friedrich Schiller was taking the theatre by storm with plays like *The Robbers* (1781), *Intrigue and Love* (1784), and *Don Carlos* (1787). New concerns and new styles were on the way, and it was possible that Goethe's creativity needed a respite to respond or adapt to these new literary directions. After his tumultuous experience with *Werther*, Goethe turned his back on print and publishing, exchanging the anonymous and turbulent reading public for a friendly coterie of like-minded listeners at court. For ten years, Goethe did not publish anything in print and instead circulated works in manuscript or read aloud at evening gatherings. As one of the initial stars of the German literary market, he had now disappeared from view.

# Longing

The drama of public fame that had brought Goethe to Weimar was replaced by yet another drama of private desire. This time the new object of Goethe's longing was Charlotte von Stein, who was married to Baron Josias von Stein, the Duke's Chief Equerry. They met after his arrival in 1775 when she was thirty-three and Goethe was twenty-six, and over the next eleven years before Goethe's departure for Italy they exchanged 1,700 letters. She was not only an important medium of temperance in Goethe's life, helping him grow out of his days of *Storm and Stress* and learn the unwritten rules of courtly life. She was also a surprisingly durable object of desire, eliciting from Goethe an unparalleled level – and longevity – of emotional outpouring. 'I feel my existence only through you, you have taught me to love myself, you have given me a home, a language, a style,' he wrote in one letter.

They exchanged rings with their initials engraved in them and over the years oscillated between the formal and informal forms of the second personal pronouns, *Du* and *Sie*, in their letters. They met for periods at a popular spa retreat, and her son, Fritz, would move in with Goethe for a time. All of this was accepted at court and by her husband. The relationship was endowed with a deep sense of purity and 'renunciation', one of Goethe's favourite words. It was, he tells her, 'the purest, truest, and most beautiful relationship' he had ever had with a woman besides his sister. Werther's brotherly love for Lotte was realised in Goethe's turbulent love for Charlotte von Stein. Fiction didn't just follow life with Goethe, but often shaped it.

Their relationship reached a high point in the years 1781 to '82, and at this point Goethe wrote to her, 'My soul has permanently grafted itself onto yours… you know that I am inseparable from you and that neither exultation nor despair can part us. I wish that there were some oath or sacrament that would also visibly and legally make me yours, how dear that would be to me.' Speculation abounds as to how chaste this relationship was. No concrete evidence exists, if there could be such a thing, that would point to a consecrated affair. It seems rather improbable, however, if not downright impossible, that a man and a woman could carry on such a passionate relationship for so long without indulging in sex. Human nature wasn't any different in the eighteenth century, even if marriage was. Indeed that marriage was so different then from now would make it even less surprising that there was an affair. But even the possibility of chastity here suggests just how powerful Goethe's need for longing was, the lengths he would go to manufacture unquenched desire. That such machinations would and could only end in disaster, well, that was just the cost of inspiration.

The shape that this inspiration could take can be seen in such renowned poems from this period as 'Erlkönig'. It was later set to music by Franz Schubert and would arguably become one of, if not the, most famous songs in the history of Western music. 'Erlkönig' was based on a Danish ballad initially titled, 'The Elf-King's Daughter', which Herder had translated for his folksong collection. Goethe changed the poem and made it about a father riding through the woods at night with his son in his arms. The son cries out that he sees someone in the woods, the father tries to calm him repeatedly, but when they arrive home the son is dead. Few poems by Goethe were as direct and arrestingly moving as this one. As we move through the son's increasingly desperate pleas, from 'Father, don't you see him?' to 'My father!

My father, now he's grabbing me!', it is impossible for the reader's mind not to become wholly absorbed by the child's terrified perspective. The true power of the poem, however, comes from Goethe's insertion of the elf-king as a speaker, endowing him with an erotic, highly aestheticised, yet ultimately sinister vocabulary:

*I love you, your form provokes me*
*If you are unwilling, then I will use force!*

As Goethe would later say, a powerful third term, which he called 'the demonic', always hung over human desire.

In the multiple, competing perspectives that were dramatised in 'Erlkönig' (between father, son, and the miniature king), one could see how Goethe's poetry continued to offer a challenge to authority. The external verification of one's views, how could this be possible? Who were we to believe here, father or son? Where was such a thing as 'objectivity' to be found? At the same time, nature was no longer aligned with the true and the good, but with much darker forces. Nature and man were *not* one, as in 'The Song of May'. Rather nature, and man's nature in particular, contained an essential element of unknowability. Goethe's own experience with desire had much to do with this poetic reevaluation. The death of the child at the end of the ballad was also about the death of childhood more generally, the way the imagination tinged by erotic fantasy marked a key passage into adulthood – and into guilt. We can see Goethe translating such fundamental Biblical stories as the Garden of Eden – about being cast out of a natural paradise and thereby acquiring sexual knowledge – into the secular form of the folk ballad.

The fallout from such poetic inspiration assumed its usual form in Goethe's life. After ten years of exchanging letters with Charlotte and seeing her regularly, Goethe would secretly depart for Italy without telling her. He claimed to keep a notebook for her, but when he returned, he eventually found someone else. This new love was a seamstress in Friedrich Justin Bertuch's artificial flower factory, and their affair provided one of the great scandals at court. She would eventually become Goethe's wife and mother of his only surviving child (in reverse order). Her name was Christiane Vulpius. Charlotte von Stein would one day tell her son, 'Goethe's image will not hang again in my room. It is too deeply buried in my heart.' Her final request was that her funeral procession not pass by Goethe's house.

Alongside Goethe's tumultuous amorous engagements and the fits and starts of writing plays, this period also witnessed the emergence of Goethe's interest in natural science, which would remain with him for the rest of his life. Scientific investigation not only provided Goethe with a necessary dose of that elusive concept of objectivity, a kind of antidote to the world of feeling that belonged to literature. It also provided an essential element of sociability. Goethe loved talking with people and learning from them. During the early years in Weimar, he met Justus Christian Loder, professor of medicine at the University of Jena, who explained to him the principles of anatomy. Goethe began amassing skeletal specimens, spent a great deal of time observing their structures, and taught anatomical drawing courses back at court. As he spent more and more time comparing the skulls of humans and animals, Goethe made what he considered to be one of the great discoveries of his life: that the human jaw had an intermaxillary bone, contrary to popular scientific opinion. Where others had seen a unique difference between man and animal, Goethe saw continuity, the traces of skeletal sutures that marked out a distinct bone. Goethe wrote up his findings and began to circulate them among leading figures in the field. His conclusions were summarily rejected. This initial experience would shape Goethe's feelings throughout the rest of his life about the new scientific 'clerisy' who refused to see what he saw with his own eyes.

Goethe's budding interest in the study of nature also lent his urge for wandering new meaning. He now studied nature as an object, not just as a source of poetic or personal inspiration. Just as his anatomical investigations had depended upon the close observation of the 'specimen', he now was hard at work collecting mineralogical specimens, too. Goethe and his pickaxe were a familiar sight in these years, and in this he was not alone. European intellectuals had begun turning with renewed energy to the study of the earth's surface, and through the work of men like George-Louis Leclerc Buffon, James Hutton, and Abraham Gottlob Werner, the earth, like the nation or man himself, was increasingly thought to be endowed with a history, one that was significantly older than the history of humankind. Such work fed into Goethe's fascination with origins and archetypes, and during a few key journeys into the Harz mountains in 1783 and '84, Goethe began a series of studies of granite rock masses. Granite was thought to be the oldest mineral, and in the seams and turbulent organisation of granite Goethe saw the possibility of great formal beauty. Where others had only seen a record of the earth's tumultuous, volcanic beginnings, Goethe saw in granite 'parts that had originated together with their totality'. Goethe would later refer to the 'gridwork' of granite as a source of all inorganic form, recalling his love of the *Gerämse*, that wooden grid, of his childhood home that marked his first initiation into the world.

In all, the ten years that Goethe lived in Weimar before leaving for Italy in 1786 was a period of rapid turns and real doubt. He was constantly asking himself what he was doing there and how long he would stay. The mobility of the intellectual elite in eighteenth-century Germany – that they could go places and that there were numerous places to go – always begged the question, Why here? The easier it was to move about, the harder it was to say why a place mattered.

On 8th June 1777 Goethe's sister, Cornelia, died at the age of twenty-six. 'With my sister I have had a great root severed which once held me to the earth. The branches above that were fed by her will surely die off too.' By that winter Goethe was seriously uncertain about himself and his future and on 9th December he attempted to hike the nearby Brocken mountain in search of a sign. The local forester had never climbed the mountain in winter. That morning the mountain lay clouded in mist and Goethe was told it was unclimbable. At around ten o'clock in the morning the weather suddenly broke, with Goethe exclaiming, 'And shall I not go up there!' Three hours later they were at the summit in a 'bright, magnificent moment', according to his diary. It seemed to him a sign from God, a confirmation of the path his life had taken. From this experience came his hymn, 'Winter Journey in the Harz', in which he first achieves that sense of a bird's-eye view, of the poet above and apart from life, which Goethe later said informed his autobiographical works. The swift, stark contrasts that the wanderer encounters between the harsh winter landscape and the 'thousand-coloured morning', between the severity of fortune's 'iron thread' and God's all-loving nature, along with the taut, unrhyming stanzas, combine in this poem to produce some of the most powerful imagery that Goethe ever composed. As he wrote to his confidante Charlotte von Stein, 'The goal of my longing has been reached.'

On 10th April 1782, Goethe was ennobled by the Imperial Court in Vienna. It was clear he could no longer stay in the Duke's garden house. He moved into a spacious home on the town square known as the Frauenplan, where he would remain for the rest of his life. It is now the site of the Goethe National Museum. Swinging between administrative life, court life, scientific investigation and the writing of poetry, plays, and novels, Goethe was trying everything and satisfied with nothing. As Schiller would later say when he met Goethe, 'Because he tries his hand at everything, he concentrates his energies on nothing.' Or as Goethe himself would write in his notes in preparation for his autobiography, 'Man has as many true as false tendencies. This is why he is an eternal martyr without true enjoyment.'

By 1785, Goethe had given up on administrative life. He began to extricate himself from court and secretly planned his long-awaited tour of Italy, the seeds of which had been sown long ago by his father's education. Goethe arranged to have his collected works published, acquiring much-needed capital for the trip. The edition was to be a mixture of previously published and new work, but the new pieces were largely just fragments. There was a sense of defeat about it. 'When I undertook to have my fragments printed, I thought I was dead,' Goethe wrote to Carl August a few months after he left. But as ever, there was also a sense of hope, a return to the literary market that was combined with a retreat from the all-consuming world of court. Maybe with a little time, and a little longing, Goethe could start over. He had already written what would become one of the most memorable poems in the German language, 'Do you know the land where the lemon-trees bloom?' and he was now ready to leave, once again with Werther's cry resounding in his head. He departed and it was not at all clear when – or if – he would come back.

# The Italian Journey

After his usual summer visit to the spa at Karlsbad, Goethe secretly headed south on 3rd September 1786. He kept a detailed record in his diary of his changing latitude. He pushed tirelessly on in his coach, enduring long bumpy days. Finally he crossed the Brenner Pass through the alps, and when he reached Lake Garda he could feel, for the first time he said, the words of Virgil coming to life. He delighted, too, in hearing the Italian language spoken, which he knew so well. Ever the natural scientist, he recorded the rock formations, the weather, and the plant life that he saw along the way. 'The fullness of the plants and fruits hanging over walls and hedges and dangling from trellises is indescribable,' he wrote. There was a tremendous sense of anticipation during this initial portion of his trip, as the excited traveller was busy making notes about what he would focus on during his trip.

From the Brenner Pass Goethe travelled to Verona and from there to Padua. In Padua, Goethe revelled in the richness of the local botanical garden, a first inkling of his sense that he was travelling to the heart of the vegetative world. But it was also here that he began to sense his loneliness, that for the first time in his entire life he was truly away from all of his social responsibilities. As he remarked when sitting in one of Padua's cathedrals, 'It was here that I truly felt alone, for no one in the world who would have thought of me in that moment would have searched for me there.'

'Thus it stood written on my page in the book of fate that on the twenty-eighth of September, evening around five o'clock, I should see Venice.' This was how Goethe recorded his entry into Venice and it was a sign of the way each of his destinations on his Italian journey would be invested with enormous personal significance. Goethe spent his time in Venice deliberately getting lost in the canals, choosing to ignore the large guidebooks that he had brought with him. He was fascinated by the engineering of the canals and the bridges, but most of all by the people or '*das Volk*'. Italy was for Goethe a constant experience of lively public life, of a seamless and harmonious public sphere, so he imagined, that moved between the theatre and the streets. Animated conversation, pronounced gestures, endless masquerades, these were all the quintessential elements of Italian popular culture and they seemed so foreign to the German courtly or even bourgeois life that Goethe had left behind.

Italy was above all, however, a world of art for Goethe. He was obsessed with the architectural work of the great Renaissance master Andrea Palladio, who was often commissioned to work for the Venetian aristocracy and who produced a signature style that integrated classical columns and staircases with the traditional forms of the aristocratic villa. As Goethe remarked, Palladio's greatness resided in his ability to combine the antithetical structural elements of the column and the wall. At the Bevilaqua Palace in Verona, Goethe saw Tintoretto's *Coronation of the Virgin* and marvelled at its multiplicity, saying one would need to look at it one's entire life to appreciate it. In Bologna, Goethe saw a portrait of St Agatha and remarked that he would not let his Iphigenia say anything that the picture of this saint would herself not have said. It was a world in which art gave birth to art, and Goethe was above all else learning to see: 'I keep my eyes permanently open and impress the objects into myself.'

On 1st November Goethe arrived in Rome, where he would stay for the next four months. It was also the first moment when he began to correspond again with his friends and colleagues back in Weimar. 'Forgive me the secret and underworldly journey here,' he says, 'but only under the Porta del Popolo was I certain of reaching Rome.' On 9th December, three months after his initial departure from Karlsbad, Goethe would receive his first reply from Weimar. It included a curt request from Charlotte von Stein asking for her letters back. On 23rd December, he received a much longer letter from her expressing a great deal of hurt about his departure. Goethe told Charlotte that he was keeping a diary just for her, which he did indeed send to her, but the break had essentially been made.

While in Rome Goethe lived an altogether different life than he had in Weimar. He went by the designation 'Filippo Möller, *pittore'*, and eschewed the high society of court in favour of the more bohemian world of ex-patriot artists. He lived with his new friend, Wilhelm Tischbein, at the Casa Moscatelli, in a spare room with a bed, table, and a few shelves that would later hold his giant plaster cast of the bust of Juno. In the morning he would work on completing his play, *Iphigenia in Tauris*, and during the day he would sightsee, visiting all the major sites of Rome: the Pantheon, the Coliseum, St Peter's Basilica, and the Sistine Chapel. *The Last Judgment* was, Goethe said, the single greatest work of art he had ever seen. In Rome he befriended the art historian Johann Heinrich Meyer, who would become a crucial correspondent of Goethe's throughout his life, as well as Angelica Kauffmann, who was one of the most famous painters in Europe and whom Goethe referred to as the 'inestimable one'. The young author, Carl Philipp Moritz, also became a close friend of Goethe's and later an important devotee. The émigrés would meet at the Café Greco to socialise and plan outings. Goethe called Rome 'the capital of the world' and it was by far the largest city he had ever seen. He was so overwhelmed by everything that he remarked, 'One has to write with a thousand pens here, what good is a single quill?'

Rome was the epicentre of his voyage to Italy, just as Italy became the epicentre of his own life. 'I count a second birthday, a true rebirth, from the day that I entered Rome,' he wrote in his diary. Goethe would later erect a monument to his time in Rome and Italy through the production of three volumes of his autobiography that were initially subtitled, 'I too was in Arcadia!', and which later came to be known as *The Italian Journey* in his final collected works edition. Italy was not only a rebirth for Goethe but also a re-education. Through its organic and artistic plenitude, it afforded him a space to rethink his own mission as an artist. 'Everything that I already knew has only just now truly become my own.' Indeed, it became the place where Goethe's emerging ideas about Art and the Artist, both with capital A's, were gradually coming into focus. If he were to return to Weimar, it could no longer be as a servant of the state, but as an Artist in the service of humanity.

During the opening weeks in Rome, Goethe was at work completing and versifying his play, *Iphigenia in Tauris*, which would go on to become one of his most important dramatic works. *Iphigenia* was an adaptation of a play by Euripides of the same name, which was based on the story of Agamemnon's daughter. Iphigenia is supposed to be sacrificed by her father to guarantee favourable winds for the Greeks to attack Troy, but she is secretly rescued at the last moment by the gods and deposited on the island of Tauris. Agamemnon's subsequent death at the hands of his wife, Clytemnestra, upon his return from battle is in part a revenge killing for this initial sacrificial murder of their daughter. Electra, Iphigenia's sister, will then coerce their brother, Orestes, into murdering their mother to avenge the death of their father, and for this transgression Orestes is plagued by the 'furies' and endures a life of wandering and madness. In order to cure himself of his madness he is told that he needs to find the image of Diana and his desperate search leads him to the island of Tauris, where he once again meets his sister. This is where Goethe's drama begins.

Or more properly speaking, it begins with Iphigenia in exile:

*Into your shade, agile boughs*
*Atop the ancient, holy, verdant grove,*
*As if among the goddess' tranquil sanctum,*
*I now step with trembling sense,*
*As though I enter for the first,*
*My spirit lies here unaccustomed.*
[...]
*I do not judge the gods; yet*
*Alone does woman's lot merit pity.*

Goethe was drawn to such tales of exile, all the more so now that he was in Italy. Like his later play *Torquato Tasso*, *Iphigenia* was an exploration of what the Romantic poet Felicia Hemans, when writing about Goethe's plays, said was the experience of 'the bitter taste of another's bread, the weary steps by which the stairs of another's house are ascended'. Iphigenia's problem was not just that she was 'unaccustomed', longing for her Greek home, but that she could not find the right balance between expressing thanks to her benefactor, the barbarian King Thoas, and preserving an intact sense of self. For a woman, such rules of reciprocity could become all too invasive: Thoas wanted to take Iphigenia as his wife.

*Iphigenia* is above all a play about sacrifice and in this it marks a major turn away from Goethe's earlier poetry about feeling and desire. Iphigenia, who has been spared once from being the victim of sacrifice, is now called on to sacrifice herself, and her body, yet again to become Thoas' wife. She is ever the child of sacrifice, her latest predicament a continuation of her own family history: not only will her family consume itself in a series of revenge murders, but she descends from the 'line of Tantalus', the mortal who secretly served his child to the gods as dinner as a way of showing them he was their equal. (His punishment was forever to want to eat a piece of fruit he could not reach, from which we get the word 'tantalise'.) This son who almost became a meal then gave birth to two sons, one of whom would one day kill his brother's children in revenge for the murder of his own son and secretly serve them as dinner to their father. This was Agamemnon's father, Iphigenia's grandfather. It was one of the most gruesome genealogies in human history.

In taking on the most infamous of all classical tales of familial revenge and sacrifice, Goethe's aim was to think through the possibility of the end of sacrifice. How could one envision a social order that did not depend on a culture of violent reciprocity – on the giving of one's entire body and being in return for some act, whether a right (as in Thoas' protection of Iphigenia) or a wrong (as in Orestes' murder of his mother)? How could one imagine a self free from debt, a truly autonomous 'I'?

This was the goal of Goethe's drama and it was in a most basic sense the apotheosis of the Enlightenment project as defined by Kant: to achieve autonomy for oneself through the use of one's own reason. But here Goethe gives us an epoch-making twist. It was not reason that was placed at the heart of this truly individual self, but beauty. Iphigenia's beauty – and in particular the beauty of her language – is what saves both Thoas and Orestes, the two principal male characters of the play. Unlike Euripides' drama in which the siblings trick the unwitting barbarian King into letting them off his island (a familiar case of Greek cleverness), in Goethe's adaptation Thoas freely grants their request. For the play to be a success, Iphigenia's plea to Thoas cannot be understood as yet another example of female guile and casuistry, but instead as a sign of truth. Her exquisite use of language in the service of enabling the ruler to pardon his subjects – to give them something without asking for something in return – is the ultimate ideal of art in an age of absolutism. Her disinterested speech marks a stark contrast to her female sibling and counterpart, Electra, who incites her brother to murder through her cunning rhetoric. As Orestes will declare towards the close of the play,

'Thus shall power and cunning, highest boast of men, be shamed by truth, the truth of *her* great soul.' Or as Goethe would write in his famous dedication to his collected edition, written before his departure to Italy:

> *Spun from the morning mist and the lucidity of the sun,*
> *Poetry's veil is taken from the hand of truth.*

Language was being reconfigured in plays like *Iphigenia* and poems like 'Dedication' not as something deceptive and unreliable, but as the highest vehicle for truth. And it would be the beautiful use of language – Art – that was the fundamental means of finding this truth. Simply put, art replaced artifice. Never before and perhaps never again would the art of language be held in such high regard. As one of the truly great dramatic poems that we have on record (it can hardly be called a play), it should remind us not to overplay the sense of creative crisis that surrounded Goethe's life during this period. Indeed, it can help us to see how much his sense of drift, exile, and giving up were integral to his periods of inspiration.

After *Iphigenia* and Rome, Goethe moved on to Naples. He marvelled at what he called the 'drunken self-abandon' of the Neapolitans, something that the extremely self-conscious author could never attain. He visited craters on Mount Vesuvius, was driven back by the fumes, but saw lava for the first time in his life. He visited Pompeii and was surprised by the modest living standards preserved there. In Naples he also met Sir William Hamilton, whose vast collection of illustrated Greek vases, which were reproduced by Tischbein, were to exert an enormous influence on nineteenth-century art. Through the work of John Flaxman, the outline drawings on the vases became a model of a new illustrative practice for book illustration that assumed great significance for a subsequent generation of Romantic artists. Goethe was also enchanted by 'Emma Hart' (aka Amy Lyon), Hamilton's future wife, who would entertain guests with the popular drawing-room game of *tableaux vivants*, where she would strike poses from famous paintings. The tension between the living reproduction and the frozen human form in the *tableaux* captured a popular fascination with art's capacity to arrest and enliven at the same time. Goethe would later memorialise this practice in his novel, *The Elective Affinities* (1809), where onlookers beg the performer, 'Turn around! Turn around!'

From Naples, Goethe made his way to Sicily, becoming terribly seasick on the several days' journey. Sicily would become both the crowning moment and the turning point of his trip. As Goethe elected not to continue on to Malta, Sicily marked an end. But it was also where Goethe imagined he had found the origin of all things. 'Italy without Sicily leaves no image in the soul: here is the key to everything.' In the Palermo gardens Goethe had his epiphany about the *Urpflanze* or 'original plant': the notion that all plant forms derived from one single form. His thinking about the origins of nature characteristically turned to thinking about the origins of antiquity. After visiting the gardens he bought a copy of Homer and would read it aloud to his travelling companion, Christoph Heinrich Kniep. Inspired by his reading, he wrote portions of a planned drama about Nausicaa, the story of a princess who brings a shipwrecked traveller to her father hoping to marry him only to find out that he then departs. It was a classic Goethean story about the continual feeling of being shipwrecked, being saved by a woman, and then contending with the aftermath of leaving her behind.

Instead of going to Syracuse, Goethe elected to head into the central region of Sicily to inspect the agricultural techniques of what was known as the breadbasket of antiquity. He then gradually made his way back to Naples. He was for the first time repeating his itinerary and sensed that he was going home. He arrived back in Rome in June 1787, but then elected to stay through the summer, which turned into a stay through the spring of the following year. In the summer of 1787 Goethe was at work completing his political drama, *Egmont*, about the sixteenth-century Dutch Count who took part in the revolt against the Spanish crown, had an affair with a simple bourgeois woman, and was later executed. It presaged things to come. In the winter Goethe had his own affair with 'Faustina', the daughter of an innkeeper who had a three-year-old child. Carl August wrote to tell him that his mother might be coming to Italy and that Goethe could be her guide: it appeared that his Italian journey might be extended for quite some time. But then his participation in that voyage was rejected and he was sternly recalled by the Duke. Goethe agreed to return, but under his own conditions. He left behind the sum of 500 Thaler for Faustina and her family under a pseudonym and began the long journey back to Weimar.

# Revolutions

On 14th July 1789, an angry mob of Parisians stormed a local prison known as the Bastille. After several hours of intense fighting a ceasefire was negotiated. The prison's warden, Bernard-René de Launay, was eventually dragged through the streets and murdered. His head was placed on a pike and paraded through the streets. The rioting, which had been ongoing through the weekend, continued and eventually spread into the provinces. French nobles began to flee the country. The National Constituent Assembly, which had been formed on 17th June to create a French constitution, decreed the end of feudalism on 4th August 1789. On 26th August, the 'Declaration of the Rights of Man and the Citizen' was issued. What later came to be known as the French Revolution had begun.

Throughout Europe all eyes were on France. Intellectuals followed the events closely through the burgeoning press and took stands both for and against. In the German territories, Kant began reading the papers regularly, Klopstock wrote an ode to the Estates General, and the young Hegel fell in with his brilliant fellow seminary students, Friedrich Wilhelm Joseph Schelling and Friedrich Hölderlin, to avidly debate the dawning of a new age in philosophy. Goethe, on the other hand, decried the rise of partisanship and the mobilisation of opinion that the press (and not art) was generating. As a lover of form, social disorder was not to Goethe's liking. 'It is in my nature,' Goethe would write many years later in his autobiography, 'that I would rather commit an injustice than endure disorder.' Despite the widespread interest in the events in France, however, the revolution remained, in the German territories at its outset, merely an affair of the press. The food shortages were less severe, the polity more fragmented, and the connection between rulers and ruled much more intimate than in France, so that there were fewer impetuses for uprising. Tensions were lower and could be diffused more quickly. There were no symbolic centres like Paris, Versailles or the Bastille that could serve as potent backdrops for greater social change. It would be several years until the Germans and German politics would be directly impacted by the events in France, but then things would be irrevocably altered.

Meanwhile back in Weimar things were changing, too, but in much different ways. Goethe had long returned from his Italian journey, and as is often the case, those who were left behind were bitter. Reintegration into courtly life was far harder than Goethe, always naive in these matters, had imagined. In August, Goethe turned forty. Life expectancy for men was thirty-eight in those days and there must have been a palpable sense of getting older. He was gradually completing his collected edition, the 'summa' of his life's work. But he also learned about another new summation, this time the result of his personal desire. One year earlier while taking a walk in the park along the Ilm, he was approached by a young woman asking for help for her brother, Christian August Vulpius. Christiane, as she was called, soon became Goethe's lover. In June the following year, during the summer of the great revolution in France, she told Goethe that she was pregnant with his child. On 25th December 1789, Christmas Day, Goethe became a father. Little August, named after his maternal uncle, and perhaps the Duke, was christened two days later in St Jacob's Church. There was no mention of the father in the church registry.

Goethe's affair with the seamstress from the artificial flower factory became public knowledge earlier in the spring and was tolerated (barely), for a time, by the members of court, including the Duke. After all, such behaviour would have been nothing new to the Duke. Even Christiane's pregnancy did not pose an insurmountable social problem. Goethe could have paid her off and set her up in a home to raise the bastard child on her own, as aristocrats so often did. But he was still too much the Frankfurter *Bürger* for that, and it was also likely that Christiane, much to the astonishment of his contemporaries, meant too much to him. On the other hand, the noble Goethe could have married her and integrated her into courtly life. This too was possible, even if uncommon. But he had fled from this possibility before and to partake in a deeply Christian ritual now seemed increasingly hypocritical to Goethe, whose Christianity had all but withered by the time he returned from Rome. Instead, he went the way of Goethe, against either of the two institutions of the nobility or the bourgeoisie. 'I am married,' he said, 'just not with a ceremony.' It was clear that becoming a father had changed him and his sense of self, and it offered him, truly for the first time in his life, a sense of fulfillment, however brief. As he would write in one of his *Roman Elegies* from this period:

*Whether what Moses and the prophets spoke*
*Was fulfilled about the sacred Christ, friends,*
*This I do not know. But this I know:*
*Fulfilled are one's wishes, desires and dreams,*
*When the lovely little child sweetly sleeps*
*Upon my breast.*

The dream of the domestic idyll that Goethe saw at the heart of human culture – a thoroughly eighteenth-century fantasy – had finally come true when he had a son.

Goethe placed Christiane, himself and the child in the Duke's hunting lodge, living apart from Weimar society in a rather bizarre arrangement. His relationships with the members of the court, which were already not on good terms since his return from Italy, were increasingly strained by this unusual arrangement. The fact that Goethe was still getting paid and had no official duties didn't help either. Besides finishing his drama about the Italian Renaissance court poet, Torquato Tasso, who eventually went mad, he was also at work composing his 'Erotica Romana', later to be called *The Roman Elegies*. They marked a new turn in Goethe's work from the sentimental to the sensual, 'to see with feeling eye, to feel with seeing hand,' as he wrote in one. They were a monument to physical union and the knowledge of desire fulfilled, ideas closely intertwined with his budding relationship with Christiane. Everything else was bracketed except the moment of encounter and one can see in this sensual immersion a further retreat from the social world of Weimar.

*I know full well how quite superfluous*
*I have long since become at court, fair friend.*

This was Tasso's curt reply to Princess Leonora in Goethe's drama, *Torquato Tasso*. In it we can see how difficult courtly life had become for Goethe and how retreat and solitude had emerged as fundamental ingredients of his own creativity. Tasso would later compare the poet to the silkworm encasing himself in his own thread.

*So in the end I see myself banished,*
*Driven away and banished like a beggar.*
*They crowned me – only to be led before the altar*
*Adorned like another sacrificial victim!*

*Torquato Tasso* was one of the most eloquent laments about the artist's awkward position in the world. 'If mankind in its torment must be mute,' says Tasso, 'some god gave me the power to tell my pain.'

While *Tasso* would be finished in time for the collected edition, *Faust* would not. Its scope was too great and Goethe did not yet have a definitive plan for it. It would have to await its time, although it would be published as a fragment. In the spring of the following year, 1790, Goethe published his new treatise on the metamorphosis of plants, inspired by his close botanical studies of the vegetation in Italy. 'Metamorphosis', a concept that had fallen out of favour in the taxonomic rage of the eighteenth century, would become an essential leitmotif to all of Goethe's thinking. Understanding the system of change – how unity and form were maintained over time through physical and spiritual development – was one of Goethe's great concerns throughout his life. In it we can see an important precursor to the Darwinian revolution of the nineteenth century.

If the study of plants and change marked one key pole of Goethe's ever-expanding scientific investigations, then his interest in the nature of colour occupied the other. For the great poet of nature, understanding colour in all of its diversity, its causes and its origins was an urgent concern, although what colour was was not something entirely clear to eighteenth-century individuals. In February, Goethe borrowed a prism from a friend and expected to see gradations of colour projected on the white wall before him, according to the most recent treatise on optics by the great European scientist, Isaac Newton. Instead, the white wall stayed white and only where an object darkened the light entering the prism (in this case the window frame) were colours projected onto the wall. For Goethe, this suggested that Newton's theory that light could be divided into the various spectrum of colours was completely wrong. Nothing seemed more anathema to Goethe, the theorist of connectivity, than that something as elemental as light was divisible. Instead, Goethe opined that it was the opposition and interaction of light and dark that produced colour. It was the *mixture* of brightness and darkness that allowed colours to emerge.

Goethe came to see this chance observation as an epoch-making epiphany. And it was all too indicative of Goethe's approach to scientific investigation: a single observation that did not correspond to received theory would instantly assume universal significance. Once fastened upon, it could not be let go of, however erroneous (as it was in this case). Attacking the Newtonian creed would prove to be a forty-year-long crusade, bordering on the deranged.

Later that spring, Goethe returned to Italy to meet the Duchess in Venice. He was disappointed by his return. It was clear just how much Italy had become an idea, not a reality, something to be internalised and then unfolded, but not revisited. After Goethe returned to Weimar, he was made the director of the new court theatre in January 1791, an activity that would consume an enormous amount of his time and interest over the next decade. The theatre was of modest size (fourteen rows of benches in a fifty-foot long room with a twenty-foot wide stage) although its initial repertory was not: it consisted of eleven operettas and thirty-five plays in the summer season alone. These consisted largely of popular dramas by August Wilhelm Iffland and August von Kotzebue, but Goethe's favourite, Shakespeare, was also introduced. Over the years, the Weimar theatre would prove to be an important opening venue for the plays of Friedrich Schiller, who would emerge as one of the great dramatists of all time.

Goethe continued to be active as the impresario of Weimar intellectual life and in that year he also founded what came to be known as the 'Friday Club', a monthly gathering of the learned that took place on the first Friday of every month. It was a delightful indication of the highs and lows of amateur intellectual life that characterised German courtly life at the end of the eighteenth century. There were readings of Johann Bode's translation of Montaigne, exhibitions of paintings by Meyer, antique urns by Böttiger, gardening by Bertuch, and of course Goethe on colour. Perhaps more importantly, it was one more vestige of that problematic notion of 'the public' that would vex Goethe and his contemporaries throughout their entire careers. Who was Goethe's audience? How could it be reached or even created? Such amateur salons were hybrids between the more professional philosophical societies and the receding world of patronage and courtly performance. In between there would gradually emerge a mass-reading audience, but its tastes were so unreliable, if not downright wretched, how was one to educate this 'public'? These coterie gatherings were an attempt to cultivate, but also perhaps to avoid, this broader and anonymous reading audience. Goethe's full commitment to the printed book as *the* forum of modern intellectual life was still in the making.

On 20th April 1792, France declared war on Austria, which had allied itself with Prussia. The French Revolution was now about to experience one of its greatest tests: an invasion by the famed Prussian military. The Duke of Weimar and his small army were called upon to accompany the campaign, and the Duke had asked Goethe to come with him. Goethe would later record his travels in his autobiographical writings, and in this we have a record of this decisive turning point in European history. By August, an army of sixty thousand men, consisting mostly of Prussians, Austrians, Hessians and French émigrés, had been assembled on the Rhine. In France, King Louis XVI had just been arrested. The allied forces began their march on Paris, first capturing Longwy and then Verdun by 3rd September 1792. On the same day, riots broke out in Paris in fear of the allied invasion. Mobs broke into Paris prisons holding priests and aristocrats, murdering hundreds and mutilating their bodies. Among the invading army there was a sense that they would reach Paris in no time at all. The exiled French aristocrats had assured their allies that the revolutionary army was not only incapable, but lacked the loyalty of the people. They would be greeted as liberators.

Nothing proved further from the truth. Intense rain slowed the allies' progress immeasurably. Carriages were constantly getting stuck, overturning, or stopping altogether from broken axles. Goethe called it the 'worst weather in the world'. One evening, when the encampment's sewage ditch overflowed, Goethe recorded, the soldiers' tents were floating in human excrement and animal carcasses. Half of the army got dysentery, Goethe included (delicately referred to in his notes as 'the universal malady'). To make matters worse, local peasants burned their supplies so that the invading army would not be able to supply itself with much-needed food during its lethargic journey.

Advancing slowly, the Duke of Brunswick intended a careful approach to Paris, perhaps encamping over the winter; the King of Prussia, Frederick William II, who was his superior, favoured a hurried onslaught to take advantage of French disorganisation. The allies made a rapid push leaving behind their logistical supply-chain. Days of hunger ensued for the troops. As they approached Valmy a dramatic series of moves by the two French generals, Charles François Dumouriez and François Christophe Kellermann, forced an encounter between the two armies where the French occupied the high ground, a ridge overlooking a valley below, which Goethe likened to an amphitheatre. The battle was in all likelihood over before it started. There ensued a day-long cannonade on 20th September 1792. Goethe described the deafening sounds of the cannons and the intensity of the sense of danger. But nothing changed. The Prussians mounted a half-hearted cavalry invasion, but it was, quite literally, an up-hill battle. The Duke of Brunswick settled on negotiating a peace settlement, ensuring his troops' safe return across the Rhine. Goethe recounted the keen sense of danger that he felt while retreating through the Argonne Forest, always waiting for French troops to ambush them. He made a pledge to himself never to be bored at the theatre again if he made it home safely.

The French had turned back the Prussian war machine and Goethe had seen just how deeply revolutionary sentiment had penetrated into the populace. As he remarked to a fellow-soldier, 'Here and now a new epoch in world history is beginning, and you will be able to say that you were there.' The Prussian retreat through the rain and mud – and even more mud – would take several weeks, with thousands dying along the way. After taking a detour down the Rhine to visit friends, Goethe finally arrived home, ecstatic to be ensconced once again in family life. On 21st January 1793, King Louis XVI of France was executed. The French Revolution had entered a new phase. The Reign of Terror was about to begin.

# The Aesthetic Education of Man, or, Schiller

If these years of Goethe's life were marked by political and personal revolutions – the events in France, becoming a father in Weimar – they were also shaped by the gradual introduction of a person into Goethe's life who would have the single most important impact on his work of anyone he would ever meet. Friedrich Schiller had arrived in Weimar in 1787 as an itinerant playwright who had been unable to find permanent employment at one of the handful of large repertory theatres in the German states. His first play, *The Robbers*, had been a tremendous sensation (on opening night audience members were literally screaming and falling out of their chairs), but he had never been capable of churning out standard bourgeois fare like Kotzebue or Iffland. Schiller was hopeful that Weimar's Privy Counsellor, the Duke's favourite, might be able to secure for him some form of permanent employment at the 'Muses' Court'. In the summer of 1788 Schiller was introduced to Goethe but received a rather cold reception. As Schiller would later write to a friend about Goethe, 'He benevolently makes his existence known, but only like a god, never giving of himself. Men should not surround themselves with this kind of being.'

Goethe's initial antipathy to Schiller is hard to gauge. Schiller was largely known as an author of plays in the style of *Sturm und Drang*, a movement Goethe had long since left behind. Physically Schiller was also extremely tall, thin and, although quite handsome, somewhat sickly, a feature that was likely to be repellent to Goethe in his post-Roman phase of searching for sensual robustness. It may simply also have been that he saw a potential rival. Schiller was extremely articulate and a rousing orator. Goethe was the keeper of courtly intellectual life. For a time, there was only room for one star.

Goethe did advocate for Schiller to receive a professorship in history at the University of Jena. But it was an unpaid position and it was not in Weimar. Schiller's inaugural lecture was attended by over three hundred students and afterwards he was paraded through the streets. No one could move a crowd quite like Schiller.

There the matter rested until several years later when Schiller attempted once again to befriend, and enlist, the *Genie* of Weimar in what would become an ambitious series of publishing ventures. The decade-long collaboration that ensued would later be dubbed the period known as *Weimarer Klassik*, dutifully force-fed to generations of subsequent German high-school students. However much of a cliché it may have become, the friendship between two such astonishingly gifted writers of very different personalities that generated such creative output is indeed remarkable in the history of literature.

In June 1794, Schiller wrote to Goethe to ask his help with a new monthly periodical he was planning called *Die Horen* (*The Horae*). Set against the backdrop of the revolution in France, its goal was nothing less than 'to unite the politically divided world under the banner of truth and beauty'. Then, on 20th July, Goethe and Schiller met by chance at a meeting of the Natural Philosophical Society in Jena and went for what would become one of the most famous walks in world literature. Along the way they began to talk about nature, about the possibility of understanding it not as something separate and individuated, but as active and vital. Goethe claimed it was only through experience that one could understand this. They soon reached Schiller's house, the conversation grew heated. Schiller was sceptical of

Goethe's claims. After declaiming portions of his treatise on *The Metamorphosis of Plants*, Goethe drew for Schiller with 'characteristic strokes' a 'symbolic plant'. Schiller shook his head and said, 'That's not experience, that's an idea.' Goethe became annoyed and replied, 'How nice that I have ideas without knowing it and can indeed see them with my own eyes.' But as Goethe would later say, the first step had been taken. Goethe, ever the believer in the importance of polarity, had found his alter-ego. 'And so we sealed,' Goethe tells us, 'an alliance through that great and infinitely unsettled contest between Subject and Object.'

Goethe agreed to participate in Schiller's periodical. In August, on the occasion of Goethe's birthday, Schiller wrote Goethe a lengthy letter about his work that was more of a literary critical essay. In September, Schiller stayed for two weeks at Goethe's home in Weimar. In deference to Schiller's disapproval of their living arrangements, Christiane and the five-year-old August remained hidden from view during the writer's stay.

Schiller's campaign to win Goethe over was a full-frontal assault – not just of flattery but also one of intellectual engagement. As in their intense conversation at Schiller's home in Jena the month before, Schiller's persistent interest in Goethe's ideas and his ability to challenge him and propel him creatively was ultimately what drove them together. Several years later Goethe would write to Schiller, 'You granted me a second youth and made me a poet once more, which I had all but ceased to be.'

At a time when the nearby sounds of war alarm the Fatherland, when the battle of political opinion renews the war in almost every circle, all too often scaring off the muses and the graces, when no salvation is to be found in either conversation or writing from the persecuting demon of political theory, it may indeed be as bold as it is useful to invite the distracted reader to an entertainment of a radically different sort.

This was the opening salvo in Goethe and Schiller's war against partisanship and the timeliness of writing, a call for 'silence about the day's favourite topic' (the French Revolution). In its stead they proposed a periodical of literature and essays to elevate readers above the day's events that would cultivate an interest in what they immodestly called the 'purely human'. A more ambitious project for a magazine one could not imagine.

Schiller opened the periodical in the winter of 1795 with a series of letters entitled *On the Aesthetic Education of Man*, one of the most important theoretical treatises ever written in the German language. It marked the result of years of reflection on the question of 'the Beautiful', because, as Schiller tells us, it was the Beautiful through which one passed on the way to 'Freedom'. Art was a way to disengage one's mind from the distractions of the day's political events, to think of something more elevated and eternal. Here we see the seeds of 'art for art's sake' being planted, the idea that experiencing art was a fundamentally disinterested activity, an idea that owed much to the work of Immanuel Kant (whom Schiller read assiduously). But Schiller's argument was also an elaborate means of bypassing the daily grind in order to arrive back at the political. The intellectual freedom that art incubated would ultimately be translated back into a form of political freedom. Art was the great edifier, not of revolutionaries, but of free and enlightened citizens. As Schiller said in the fourth letter, 'Man in time will be ennobled into Man in the Idea.'

Alongside Schiller's letters, Goethe published *Conversations of German Refugees*, a novella cycle based on Boccaccio's *Decameron* (c. 1353) that also recycled and rewrote stories from other collections. Ever the great consumer of the vast history of the world's literatures, Goethe once again resurrected a genre and an author who had lain dormant for centuries (at least for German readers).

And like Schiller's letters, it addressed the newfound sense of the rupture of community and suggested that reparation was only possible through the creation of new forms of communication. Only the veil of art – the way it delayed instant gratification – could restore the political fragmentation of European culture. *Conversations of German Refugees* would establish an obsession with the 'novella' among subsequent German writers that would stretch from the likes of Romantics such as E.T.A. Hoffmann and Ludwig Tieck to the great modernists Franz Kafka and Thomas Mann.

When Schiller had initially invited Goethe to participate in the *Horen* project, he had hoped Goethe would give him portions of his new novel in progress, *Wilhelm Meister's Apprenticeship*. After eight years, Goethe had returned to this fragment and had, with much input from Schiller, begun vigorously transforming and expanding it. Never before in Goethe's life, and indeed never after, had another author had such a significant impact on the making of one of his works.

Published in four volumes in the same year as the *Horen* opened, *Wilhelm Meister's Apprenticeship* was a massive, inchoate work of literature. It made Henry James's later epithet for the novel – 'loose baggy monsters' – appear decidedly understated. There were sultry actresses, gypsy circus performers, beautiful amazons, a crazy, pyromaniac harpist, revelations of incest, abandoned children, and a secret society that monitored the course of Wilhelm's life and recorded it all in a book. It contained some of Goethe's finest poems and the famous 'Confession of a Beautiful Soul' that was based on the life of his Frankfurt mentor, Susanne von Klettenberg. The novel was about Wilhelm's journey of joining and then leaving behind the theatre as the essential artistic medium, about abandoned lovers (of course), about overcoming class distinctions between the bourgeoisie and the aristocracy, but most of all it was about a confused young man making his way in the world who in the end says, 'I have nothing to recount about my life except one mistake after another.'

The *Apprenticeship* would later become known as the first *Bildungsroman*, a difficult concept to translate that means something like a novel about the development and acculturation of the individual. Of course it wasn't really the first and it wasn't even necessarily a *Bildungsroman*, but it was a major sensation for German readers. As the up-and-coming Romantic theorist and essayist, Friedrich Schlegel, would quip, 'The French Revolution, Fichte's *Theory of Knowledge*, and Goethe's *Meister* are the three greatest tendencies of the age.' Schlegel would later write a long essay on Goethe's novel and this, along with his 'Letter on the Novel', would prove to be an immensely influential theorisation of the genre for future writers. Goethe's novel captured the challenges of what it meant to live in a society defined by upward mobility instead of one where your lot in life was determined from birth. It depicted in brilliant, eclectic detail the haphazard quest for individuality and meaning that had come to inform Europeans' sense of self at the close of the eighteenth century. Unlike Meister's famed predecessor, Don Quixote, who was in search of values long since gone that he had read about only in books, Wilhelm Meister was in search of himself – and more importantly, the possibility of cultivating his best self.

If *Wilhelm Meister's Apprenticeship* proved to be an enormous success, the *Horen* was not. It folded just two years later in 1797. In response to the numerous critiques that it had endured – largely charges of being too elitist and not entertaining enough – Goethe and Schiller contrived to produce a bilious counterattack. In the *Muses' Almanac* for 1797, which Schiller edited (he was nothing if not industrious), the accomplices produced 400 stinging distichs about contemporary German writers, professors and publishers, which were called, *Xenien*, a Germanised Greek word meaning a gift presented by a guest. Gifts indeed. As Schiller wrote to Goethe about the literary public, 'One has to discomfort them, disturb their ease, agitate and astonish them. Poetry must confront them in one of two ways, either as genius or as a spectre.' Few were spared in this literary onslaught, which in turn engendered numerous replies in print. Where the *Horen* had claimed to stand above the fray, the *Xenien* undertook one of the most familiar tactics of garnering media attention: the journalistic war.

One year later in the *Almanac*, Goethe and Schiller retreated and returned to their former ways by printing a number of poetic ballads in what came to be known as 'the year of the ballad'. In this return to what Goethe called the '*Ur-Ey*', or 'Original Egg', of all poetic genres, the duo was once again trying to find ways to transcend the popular precisely by using popular poetic forms. The ballad, we remember, was what Goethe had collected with Herder in his time riding through the Alsatian countryside twenty years earlier, and Goethe and Schiller once again returned to the ballad to negotiate between the high and the low of an incipient popular mass culture. It was a move circulating throughout Europe: that same year would see the publication of Wordsworth and Coleridge's literary experiment of the *Lyrical Ballads*. In Goethe and Schiller's project, we can see how Goethe's most famous contribution, 'The Sorcerer's Apprentice', not only reflected how important the concept of 'apprenticeship' had become to his writing – that art, like anything worthwhile, was something that you had to spend years learning. As a story about a young man who conjured up spirits and then forgot the magic word to get them to leave, it was also a wry commentary on the journalistic wars he and Schiller had recently unleashed.

In the summer of 1797, Goethe made preparations for another trip to Italy. But much had changed. He was now a father and de facto a husband. The dream of Italy was countered by the comforts of home. He departed with mixed feelings. After several days spent observing the falls of Schaffhausen – where he marvelled at the chromatic variety of the plunging water, a vision that would later assume tremendous significance in his *Faust* – Goethe chanced upon a tree wrung with ivy. It became one of those all-important pregnant moments in Goethe's life.

Like all of his epiphanies, it depended upon a powerful symbol coalescing in an instant before his eyes. And as always, it yielded beautiful poetry. 'Amyntas', not one of Goethe's most famous works but conceptually one of his most important, was a poem about a young man who tries to cut the ivy off a tree and the tree asks him to stop. 'Should I not love the plant,' asks the tree in a rather wry rhetorical question, 'that, in need of me, quietly coils itself around me?' The vine of family had encircled the trunk of the poet's self and it had taught him the bitter sweetness of domestic life. It had allowed Goethe to envision a wholly new model of artistic creativity.

On 23rd September 1797, from a village in Switzerland, Goethe wrote to Christiane:

> Now I have to add something in my own hand and tell you: that I sincerely, tenderly and only love you and that I deeply wish for nothing else than that your love for me will always remain the same. My trips won't amount to much in the future if I cannot take you with me. Even now I would prefer to be back with you, to tell you good night and good morning in our green alcove and receive my breakfast from your hand.

A few weeks later Goethe would ascend the Gotthard Pass – the crossing point of the alps into Italy – and taking one last look on his beloved Italy, he turned around.

In 1799, at the dawn of the next century, Goethe turned fifty. In that year Schiller finally moved from Jena to Weimar, bringing the two collaborators closer together. In France Napoleon would stage his coup d'état, eventually crowning himself Emperor. Meanwhile, Goethe had become the director of the ducal library and had bought an estate. He spent his evenings reading to his son and looking together with him at prints or illustrated books. During the day, he would complain about the noise, whether it was the barking of dogs or the hum of nearby looms.

In the years that followed, Goethe largely stayed in Weimar and Jena. Instead of travelling, he translated. The adaptation and dissemination of foreign literature became an increasingly important fact of his life and work. First a translation of Diderot's writings on painting, then Voltaire's *Mahomet*, a translation of the Renaissance artist Benvenuto Cellini's autobiography, and finally a translation of Diderot's *Rameau's Nephew*, which had never before appeared in print. The manuscript had been found by a friend of Schiller's in the royal library in St Petersburg and smuggled back to Weimar. Two decades later, when *Rameau's Nephew* first appeared in French, it was actually a translation of Goethe's translation into German. Another artistic periodical was started, *Propylaea* (which means 'Entryway'), this time with Goethe's friend Johann Heinrich Meyer. He composed his last drama, *The Natural Daughter*, which contained some of the most beautiful verse lines he ever wrote, and continued working on his major scientific treatise, *The Theory of Colours*, and his dramatic poem, *Faust*.

By the winter of 1805, both Goethe and Schiller had become seriously ill. Goethe very gradually improved, Schiller did not. On 9th May, Schiller died of an infection to the lung. Over the course of their decade-long friendship, Goethe and Schiller had written one another over a thousand pages of correspondence. Throughout all of their letters, Goethe never used the informal *Du* (you) with Schiller, and Schiller only mentioned Goethe's wife, Christiane, once. But they did discuss some of the most urgent concerns of how to make great works of art. Their letters are a monument to the writer's laboratory. In keeping with his general dread of death, Goethe did not attend his friend's funeral.

# The Demonic Age

On the morning of 14th October 1806, French troops administered a devastating blow to the Prussian army in the nearby
cities of Jena and Auerstädt. By the afternoon, Prussian soldiers
were fleeing through Weimar and French troops were arriving
in search of lodging. The Revolution had become palpable even
for the residents of sleepy Weimar. Goethe and Christiane had
taken in some Alsatian hussars and were designated to house the
soon-to-arrive Marshal Ney. That night there was a knock on the
door. Goethe greeted two drunken soldiers in his rather majestic
nightgown and offered them something to drink. After a while
Goethe took his leave, intending to go back to bed. The soldiers
followed and then threatened his life. Christiane suddenly
arrived with one of the Alsatians – apparently throwing herself
in front of her husband to protect him – and together they
chased the intruders into a room and locked the door. The next
morning the Marshal arrived and the soldiers were beaten and
tossed out. Ten days later, Berlin, the capital of the Prussian
state, surrendered to Napoleon.

The capitulation of Prussia marked the conclusion of a series
of dramatic events that had forever altered the European map.
Just two months earlier, on 6th August 1806, the Holy Roman
Empire of the German Nation – that ungainly political amal-
gamation that had been in existence since the tenth century –
had been dissolved. There was a deeply felt sense for Goethe that

the world was changing for good around him. Fearing for his own welfare and that of his family, Goethe resolved to formally marry Christiane. Five days later, on 19th October, they were married. On their wedding bands Goethe inscribed the date of 14th October – the day of the defeat of Jena.

If the preceding days, months, and years had marked major reorganisations to the political map of Europe, so too to the world of arts and ideas. This revolution came to be known as Romanticism and its European birthplace was the nearby university town of Jena. In the fall of 1798, the brothers August Wilhelm and Friedrich Schlegel began editing a biannual journal by the name of the *Athenaeum* that would mark the opening salvo in the decades-long battle between the Romantics and the Classicists. It was here, in a series of brilliant fragments, that Friedrich Schlegel gave voice to the new artistic sensibility that would begin coursing throughout the continent. 'Romantic poetry,' said Schlegel, is 'a progressive universal poetry.' It is still under way, 'indeed that is its fundamental essence: that it can only ever become and not be complete.'

The Schlegels were part of a fluid circle of creative minds who frequented Jena over the next couple of years and who were largely drawn there through the advocacy and influence of Goethe. After Schiller came Johann Gottlieb Fichte, the next disciple of Kantian philosophy and a brilliant orator. In addition to the Schlegel brothers there was Friedrich Schlegel's wife, Dorothea Veit, who was the daughter of the philosopher Moses Mendelssohn and who divorced a banker in Berlin to be with her new lover. There was August Wilhelm's wife, Caroline Böhmer, who was several years his senior and had been a strong supporter of the revolutionary cause in Mainz. She had had a child out of wedlock with a French lieutenant before marrying August and then left August a few years later for the philosopher Friedrich Schelling, who had assumed the chair of philosophy at Jena. There was Ludwig Tieck, who was fast becoming famous as one of the great new writers of his generation and whose daughter was one of the most talented translators in an age of great translators. And then there was Friedrich Hardenberg, also known as Novalis, the only poet who rivalled Friedrich Schlegel's aphoristic wit and who had fallen in love with a twelve-year-old; and finally, Clemens Brentano, a gifted student who would soon begin an affair with and later marry the poet, Sophie Mereau, who also lived in Jena. The social and sexual liberty of intellectual life in Jena was part and parcel of the theory of Romanticism as a fundamental challenge to convention. It embodied in both the intellectual and sensual sense Schlegel's idea of what he punningly called *Symphilosophie* – creativity grounded in community.

Out of this incestuous small-town milieu, Romanticism came to be a European phenomenon. It prized categories like irony, play, self-reflection, the fragmentary, and the ineffable. Romanticism marked the end of rules and an explosion of forms. It captured what the scholar Gerhard Neumann has called a 'post-Cartesian' sense of self, the perspectival nature of all knowledge. Truth was no longer 'out there' but crucially 'in here'. As Novalis remarked, 'The path of mystery leads into the interior.' The imagination emerged as the highest of all faculties, the mind something that we could no longer completely control nor oversee. Poetry was the science of this new cognitive uncertainty. It is easy to see how Freud's theory of the unconscious would emerge from his attentive readings of the German Romantics.

Romanticism was a movement that lasted a long time but was grounded in a sense of transience. Romanticism was about longing and burning out. Whether it was the poet Novalis who died at the age of twenty-nine, the painter Philipp Otto Runge who died at the age of thirty-three, the *Wunderkind* Karoline von Günderrode who committed suicide (with Heinrich von Kleist) at the age of twenty-six, or English icons like Lord Byron who died at thirty-six on the shores of Greece, John Keats who died at twenty-six, or the great Romantic icon and forger, Thomas

Chatterton, who poisoned himself with arsenic, Romantics always seemed to die early. As Théophile Gautier would remark in hindsight, 'In the Romantic Army, as in the army of Italy, everyone was young.'

Whatever else it was, in both its emergence and its aftermath Romanticism crucially depended on the figure of Goethe. It was Goethe who brought so many of the young Romantics to Jena and it was Goethe who was the idol of the new generation. The Schlegels would dedicate the *Athenaeum* to him, 'the true vicar of the spirit of poetry on earth'. Or as Joseph von Eichendorff, a later poet of the Romantic school, would write, 'There are certain words that, like a lightning bolt, bring forth a garden of flowers within my deepest recesses, like memories fingering the strings of my soul's Aeolian harp – words like: longing, spring, love, home, Goethe.' Over time, Goethe would become highly critical of the direction that Romanticism took: 'I call the classic healthy,' he commented to his secretary, 'and the romantic sickly.' But during these early years, he couldn't get enough of his time in Jena and the circle he cultivated there, treating the local inn as a writer's bachelor pad.

If it had been Goethe's *Wilhelm Meister* novel that initiated much of the local German Romantic fascination with Goethe, it was his great dramatic poem, *Faust*, the first part of which was published in 1808, that would become the key reference point for subsequent generations of Romantic writers across Europe and the Atlantic. Like Homer's *Iliad*, Dante's *Divine Comedy*, Shakespeare's *Hamlet*, or James Joyce's *Ulysses*, Goethe's *Faust* belonged to that constellation of works that indelibly changed the course of Western literature.

*Faust* was an adaptation of a fifteenth-century chapbook that recounted the story of a scholar who sold his soul to the devil in return for absolute knowledge of the world. It was a perfect allegory for the coming age of science. It occupied Goethe for seventy-five years and took the form of four different versions:

as an early manuscript (1773–5), a published fragment (1790), a completed 'Part I' (1808), and then 'Part II' which was only published after his death (1832). It would eventually contain 230 characters and thirty-seven different kinds of metre. Devils, earth spirits, Helen of Troy, child murder, and even debauched orgies on mountaintops – it was all in there along with some of the most stunning lines of poetry ever written in German. It contained so many kinds of poetry and so many references to other literary works that someone once said if you lost the entirety of Western literature except *Faust* you would be able to piece it all back together again.

*Faust* begins with the scholar alone in his narrow, book-lined study. He is despondent. He has learned everything, but feels he knows nothing. His famous opening monologue begins:

*I've studied now Philosophy*
*And Jurisprudence, Medicine, –*
*And even, alas! Theology,–*
*From end to end, with labor keen;*
*And here, poor fool! with all my lore*
*I stand, no wiser than before.*

He will be brought to the brink of suicide, saved by the sound of Easter bells pealing from a nearby church and conjuring powerful memories from his childhood. Time and memory are man's first redemption. The devil will be his second.

Soon Faust will conjure the devil's helper, Mephistopheles, and make the infamous wager: in return for a lifetime of unlimited pleasure, experience, and knowledge, were Faust ever to say 'enough' and be satisfied the devil will receive Faust's soul for all eternity. So long as he never ceases to strive then Faust's place in heaven is assured. Mephistopheles called himself 'the spirit who eternally negates', and he was the embodiment of the new Romantic fascination with the ineffable and the incomprehensible, what Keats would have called our 'negative capability'. As for Keats, negation for Goethe was a necessary component of creation. Like Milton's Satan in *Paradise Lost*, Mephisto has all the best lines. He articulates the deeply felt conviction on the part of the author of the absurdity of human life, a deeply comic and pessimistic figure at the same time.

Faust's dream is not to know nature in its entirety, but to understand nature in our relation to it. It is not a manifesto of raw empiricism, but instead a reflection on how our senses and our minds participate in the comprehension of the natural world. It is a search to understand the status of those 'wavering shapes' that Goethe invoked in his dedication to *Faust*, the phantasmagoric (and orgiastic) world of ethereal figures atop the Brocken during the Walpurgis Night. How we seize on that which we see, how we arrest the time of experience with our minds and give those experiences distinct mental shapes, how knowledge is comprised of a composition of perspectival parts – these are the key questions about the foundation of human knowledge that matter in *Faust*.

The major alteration Goethe made to the original myth was the addition of Gretchen, the virgin with whom Faust will one day fall passionately in love. Desire was at the heart of this new way of thinking about knowledge, and Gretchen was its symbol. Our senses, our drives, our bodies shaped what we could know about the world and how we could know it. For the poet who would never stop falling in love with young women until the day he died, desire was everything. As Faust would later say:

*Thus in desire I hasten to enjoyment,*
*And in enjoyment pine to feel desire.*

With the help of Mephisto, Faust will quickly succeed in seducing Gretchen, who is the first woman he passes on the street after drinking a magic potion. No Helen of Troy, she is a kind of everywoman. Caught up in her affair, Gretchen accidentally murders her mother one evening by giving her the devil's sleeping potion. Her brother will be killed in a duel to defend her honour, and she will become pregnant and then murder her own child, for which she is in the end imprisoned and sentenced to death. Faust's desire brings with it a long wake of death and destruction. Gretchen is the necessary sacrifice – the unavoidable outcome if you will – of understanding knowledge as grounded in the human body. The first part ends with Faust's visit to Gretchen in a dungeon. As Faust is dragged away by Mephisto, we hear a voice that pronounces Gretchen's judgment and her salvation.

If *Faust* was the fictional embodiment of the new century's fascination with the demonic, then Napoleon was his real-world counterpart. No historical actor exerted more fascination on his contemporaries than Napoleon. In his ability to change history itself he came to embody the heroic individuality that was so prized by the Romantic spirit, just as he revealed its destructive substrate. Such demonic individuals, Goethe said, exuded a 'monstrous force'. In the same year that *Faust* appeared on the literary market, Goethe would meet Napoleon. Weimar's literary Emperor was invited to meet Europe's political Emperor in nearby Erfurt over one of the more famous breakfasts in literary history. Upon seeing the old poet, Napoleon is said to have remarked, '*Voilà un homme.*' Goethe had to stand while Napoleon ate breakfast and conducted business. They talked of classical tragedy and *Werther*, which Napoleon had supposedly read a number of times. Napoleon, Goethe said, offered insightful critiques of his youthful novel. Shortly after their meeting, Goethe was awarded the French legion of honour. It was a way of enticing him to come to Paris and write a Caesar play about Napoleon. Goethe politely declined, but he would wear his medal for the rest of his life with great pride.

# New Science, New Life

By the time Goethe met Napoleon, much was passing away in his life. Not only Schiller, but also his friend Herder had recently died, as had the great poet of the eighteenth century, Friedrich Klopstock. But despite these losses, Goethe began to find new work, new relationships, and new loves in the years to come. As his friend and confidant, Karl Friedrich Reinhard, would say about him at this age, 'His stature is long and lean; one sees he has lost his *embonpoint* [stoutness]. Only his eyes now retain their restrained radiance that shines forth in the moment he laughs and then one unmistakably sees the rogue looking back at you... I have seen him warm up and heard his inner fullness brewing. I recognise the lion by his claws.'

Goethe's social life during these years is centred around the salon of Johanna Schopenhauer, mother of the philosopher Arthur Schopenhauer (*The World as Will and Representation*) and highly regarded author in her own right. On Thursday and Sunday evenings there are gatherings to hear concerts, see performances, or listen to readings. Goethe is of course one of the favourites. As Schopenhauer wrote to her son, 'Goethe himself reads at our home and to hear and see him during these readings is magnificent. No sooner has he read three pages than his poetic spirit is awakened: then he interrupts himself at every line and thousands of exquisite ideas stream forth in luscious abundance so that one forgets everything and listens only to that remarkable man.'

In the summers Goethe would begin travelling to the baths at Karlsbad, leaving Christiane and August at home. Karlsbad was a glamorous resort destination for high society. But it also afforded Goethe time away from his institutional duties to write and reflect. 'What Jena was for me, Karlsbad will be in the future,' Goethe wrote to Christiane during his visit in 1807. 'One can live here either among society or completely alone, as one wishes, and I can find here everything that interests me and gives me joy.' After Karlsbad, Goethe began a new diet: a mixture of tea and wine in the evenings, and in the morning, spa water (mineral water) mixed with either coffee, hot chocolate or broth. There was a new sense of measurement and moderation. Karlsbad was also the site of Goethe's renewed interest in all things geological, as he would make numerous excursions to surrounding areas in the summers that followed to observe rock formations. Not quite sixty, Goethe continued to stay abreast of the most recent developments in the new science of geology, always ready to weigh in on debates about the aquatic or volcanic origins of the earth's surface.

If geology continued to be a point of interest in Goethe's scientific investigations, it was the field of optics and colour theory that most thoroughly occupied him during the coming years. It was work that bordered on an obsession. 'What is the freedom of the press,' Goethe declaimed, 'for which everyone cries and sighs so insistently, if I am not allowed to say that Newton deceived himself as a young man and then spent his whole life perpetuating this self-deception!' It was always about Newton. Goethe would eventually produce a massive three-volume work, *The Theory of Colour*, to contradict Newton's findings, the first volume of which included nothing less than a history of the entire field of optics. One could only find the new, so Goethe's thinking went, by understanding just how indebted ideas were to the old and then clearing away all of those long-held assumptions. As Goethe would say, 'The history of science is science.'

All of this experimental work would soon make its way into Goethe's art. On the morning of 17th May 1807, at 6.30 a.m., Goethe began dictating his novel, *Wilhelm Meister's Travels*, with the words, 'In the shade of an imposing cliff sat Wilhelm...' It was a grandiose gesture that conjured up references to both the Bible and Plato. Where the Bible had begun with God's command, 'Let there be light!', Goethe's novel began in the shade, that all important space where he imagined colour to emerge. And where Plato's philosopher sat in a cave looking at a shadow on the wall, Goethe's hero sat outdoors in the shade looking at the prime site of geological knowledge, the cliff. The *Travels* was the story of a middle-aged man and his son who were travelling through Europe en route to founding a colony in America. Along the way the characters discuss a vast spectrum of topics: myth, history, religion, the arts, commerce, medicine, geology, pedagogy, cosmology, politics, and colonialism. The passage through space is always the passage through ideas. Goethe is concerned with representing the integration of all fields of knowledge, and the task of the novel's hero, Wilhelm, who will one day become a surgeon and save his son's life, is ultimately to learn how to combine rather than divide. It is Goethe's novel of everything and has most often been compared to Joyce's *Ulysses*. The *Travels* is one of the great experimental novels in literary history.

It would take Goethe over twenty years and two different versions to complete this last novel. This was nothing compared to *Faust*, but it was indicative of just how processual Goethe's writing was. Nothing was ever finished. What was unique about the *Travels*, however, was the way it engaged with the burgeoning world of the printed book. Diffused in numerous different formats and forms over two decades, it became a key witness to Goethe's thinking about print, publication and a public founded on reading books.

That autumn, after Goethe returned from Karlsbad, he once again began spending time in Jena. He had found another family to idealise, this time that of the publisher Carl Friedrich Frommann, whose eighteen-year-old foster daughter, Minna Herzlieb, Goethe would soon fall in love with. Once again, *amour* would be the starting point for Goethe's creativity. In December of 1807, he began composing a sequence of sonnets, which he referred to as his 'Minna-Lieder', a pun on the German medieval word for love songs, 'Minnelieder'. They were met with remarkable outpourings of sentiment when Goethe read them aloud. 'Some evenings, when I would return to my room,' Minna wrote to a friend, 'and everything was still around me, I would remember the golden words that I had heard from his mouth that evening, and I would think about what man is capable of making of himself – then tears would come streaming down my face.'

Goethe's sonnets were part of an age-old poetic tradition that dated back to Petrarch's sonnets to Laura or Dante's to his beloved Beatrice. But unlike Goethe's earlier *Roman Elegies* and their unrestrained praise of sensuality, Goethe's sonnets were much more about renunciation, distance, and the mediation of desire. The female addressee will fall in love with not the poet himself, but the poet's marble bust. The poet is mythologised but also made inaccessible. As a genre, the sonnet was in many ways the purest articulation of restraint – the most rule-bound of all poetic forms – and Goethe used it to explore a new sense of life that derived its strength from the joyful acceptance of such limitations. The opening sonnet, 'Powerful Surprise', would end with the image of a river being damned by a falling rock and the stars intermittently reflecting themselves back to the heavens in the waves crashing against the canyon's walls. Its final words were, 'A new life'.

Minna Herzlieb was not the only object of such restrained desire, nor the only addressee of the sonnets. Goethe would send his sonnets to Bettina Brentano, sister of the romantic poet Clemens, asking her to write him in return so that he would have more to 'translate', he said. She was a frequent visitor to the

Goethes' home, doting, eccentric, and extremely flirtatious. She would claim to have slept with Goethe's supposed illegitimate child, whom, she asserted, he had had with Lili Schönemann. Later, she produced a homage to Goethe by collecting their letters together in a volume called *Correspondence with a Child*, although despite its title, Bettina was anything but a child. She and Christiane would one day have a great fight and Bettina was banned from the house, along with her husband Achim von Arnim. Goethe would later say he was glad to get rid of the 'nutcases'. Bettina would go on to play an important inspirational role in the lives of numerous nineteenth-century musicians such as Beethoven and Robert Schumann, a Romantic prototype of the subsequent modernist muse, Lou-Andreas Salomé.

The following summer of 1808 Goethe would begin work in Karlsbad on yet another fictional experiment infused with ideas from his scientific investigations, *The Elective Affinities*. A tightly knit tale of a foursome who swap lovers, which drew on ideas from the field of chemistry, *Elective Affinities* was a reflection on the powers of imagination and the patterning of social behaviour. The fictional heroine, Charlotte, will one day give birth to a child who does not look like its parents, but instead like the two lovers that she and her husband were fantasising about at the moment of conception. This 'monstrous birth' will then drown towards the close of the novel, a sign of the transgression that brought it into the world. But it is also a sign of how fleeting such imaginary projections are. The mind's wavering shapes cannot last. Ottilie, the young woman that Charlotte's husband, Eduard, has fallen in love with, will then die by starvation at the end of the novel. Eduard too will expire and be buried next to her. The tale of switching lovers and older men falling in love with younger women would be explored again later to great effect in Goethe's novella, *The Man of Fifty*, which Thomas Mann considered one of the greatest novellas in German literature.

That autumn Goethe's mother would pass away, the last of his remaining nuclear family. Remaining in Weimar, Goethe avoided yet another funeral. It soon became apparent to him that it was time to reflect on his life in its entirety and to produce his much anticipated memoirs. Over the course of the next few years Goethe would produce the initial portions of his autobiography, *Poetry and Truth*, an aptly chosen title for this stylised portrait of the poet's life that would go on to become a landmark in the genre of autobiography. By the time of his final collected edition, Goethe's autobiographical writings would swell to eleven volumes of the entire edition. Few authors worked as assiduously as Goethe did to promote the author's life as the ultimate source of meaning for his works. As he would write in *Poetry and Truth*, 'Everything that I have written to this point are just fragments of a greater confession.' Or as he stated even more flatly in his aphorisms, 'Why does everyone envy the poet? Because his nature necessitates communication, indeed, his nature is the communiqué itself.' According to Goethe, the poet was the message. The autobiography would become one piece of an increasingly elaborate machine in the coming decades that would contribute to the making of *Mythos Goethe*.

In the summer of 1812, Goethe would spend much of his time in the company of the celebrated new composer, Ludwig van Beethoven. 'I have never seen an artist more composed, energetic, and introverted. I can well understand how he relates to the world in a rather astounding fashion,' Goethe wrote home to his wife. He was fascinated by this quintessential representative of the new avant-garde in the arts, recognising, without completely appreciating, the implications of Beethoven's art and the world that produced him. Remarking on how he found his music 'quite mad', Goethe shuddered, 'One feared the whole house might collapse.' In shuddering through the younger musician's extraordinarily innovative and daunting work, the older poet seemed not to recognise just how experimental and unaccommodating his own work had become. But Beethoven was just one more sign of the dramatic ways that all things – arts, ideas, and politics – were changing at the dawn of the new century. That summer Napoleon began his fateful attack on Russia.

# Mecca

On 14th September 1812, Napoleon's *Grande Armée* captured Moscow. It was a Pyrrhic victory. The Russian countryside had been decimated and now the Russians were prepared to burn their capital to the ground in defiance of foreign occupation. The 'Great Retreat' began, with fewer than a hundred thousand troops making it back to French soil, less than a third of those who started out. That spring, the allies re-entered the war sensing imminent French defeat. Over the course of that year the two sides mustered close to a million soldiers on each side, a mobilisation of troops never before seen on European soil, but one that presaged an almost apocalyptic future to come in the twentieth century. After a series of defeats in the fall of 1813, the allies eventually entered Paris on 30th March 1814. On 6th April, Napoleon Bonaparte abdicated.

In September, the famed Congress of Vienna was convened to redraw the map of Europe. The time-honoured practice of European diplomacy – civilly discussing the fates and boundaries of nations from the comfort of Rococo board rooms – was overseen in this instance by the likes of Talleyrand from France, Metternich from Austria, Hardenberg from Prussia, the Duke of Wellington from Britain and a host of other European diplomats. Besides the political gerrymandering, there also emerged a growing consensus around the need for the greater control of public speech. The so-called Carlsbad Decrees, which severely limited public political expression and reinstituted a strict regime of censorship, were passed. 'Curators' were appointed to universities to relieve politically suspect professors of their duties, student societies were disbanded, and any publication under 320 pages needed to go first through a central Censor's Bureau. Depending on one's point of view, the Congress either produced a hundred years of peace or sold out the social and political gains that were the legacies of the French and American Revolutions. For Goethe, summering in Karlsbad, it meant nothing at all: 'The fact that Moscow has burned is of no concern whatever to me. It will only provide history with something to write about.'

In the summer of 1814, just prior to the great political event of the new century, Goethe would travel to the Rhine region to observe the exquisite art collections of the Brothers Boisserée. It marked the first of a series of what Goethe would call his 'crusades', culminating in the creation of a new periodical entitled *On Art and Antiquity*. It was a response to the growing nationalistic tendency in the arts, a way for Goethe to take a genuine interest in the history of Germanic art and integrate it within the *longue durée* of the arts since antiquity. As Goethe wrote, his periodical was meant to be an educational tract for the Germans because unlike the English or the French they could not go to one single destination for their personal aesthetic education. The German art lover had to be a traveller. The medium of the book was to serve those who did not have the means to indulge in the art junket.

That summer also marked Goethe's budding interest in the poetry of the fourteenth-century Persian poet, Hafez. Goethe had avidly been reading the new publication, *Treasures of the Orient*, edited by Joseph von Hammer-Purgstall, as well as Hammer-Purgstall's translation of Hafez's work. A new Orientalism was in the air, from Friedrich Schlegel's Sanskrit studies, Washington Irving's travels to the Alhambra and a fascination with Muslim Spain, to Byron's donning of Turkish costume for one of his more famous portraits, to an emerging fascination with Egyptian hieroglyphics that was fuelled by the discovery of the Rosetta Stone in 1799, and that eventually led to its decoding by Jean-François Champollion in 1822. Goethe was drawn to this early record of Middle Eastern poetry because of the sensuality and the simplicity of its self-expression, the way it led us back, as he said in his notes, to the intersections of Jewish, Christian, and Islamic cultures and the founding documents of human civilisation.

Out of this reading gradually emerged Goethe's own collection of poems, which he entitled *The West-East Divan*; it was part translation, part rewriting of Hafez's poetry. As he remarked in his commentary to the collection, 'Ideally the author of these poems would like to be seen as a traveller.' Goethe was never far away from Werther's youthful cry, 'How happy I am to be away!', even in old age. The opening poem to the collection was called 'Hegire', which was a French transcription of the Arabic, 'Hiǧra', referring to Mohammed's flight from Mecca to Medina in the year 622. Divided into twelve books, *The West-East Divan* was not only about the importance of imaginative travel to other cultures. It was also an extended engagement with figures of cultural circulation more generally, from the nature of Middle Eastern scripts, to the spiral-like shape of the turban, to the all-important dust that accompanied the caravan and that communicated the free-floating nature of ideas as well as their inherently fleeting nature. In the collection's explosive opening lines,

*North and West and South asunder,*
*Thrones burst, empires thunder*

one could hear the splintering of cultural boundaries and a new orientation of time and space being ushered in. It was Goethe's latest salvo in what he later called a campaign to promote the idea of *Weltliteratur*, or 'World Literature'.

Goethe's turn to the East was not simply a matter of reading. Once again, there was a woman. In September 1814, Goethe met and later fell in love with Marianne Pirngruber, the thirty-year-old daughter of an Austrian actress who was living with the wealthy Frankfurt banker Johann Jakob von Willemer. Willemer would eventually marry his companion, perhaps on the advice of Goethe who had done the same with Christiane. Goethe and Marianne saw one another again the following autumn in Wiesbaden and then in Heidelberg. Knowing about Goethe's interest in Hafez, Marianne brought Goethe a poem inspired by the Persian poet. On the night of Goethe's departure for Weimar, aware that he would never see her again, he wrote what would become one of the most famous poems of his entire career, 'Ginkgo Biloba'. It was based on the tree by that name, whose distinctive fan-shaped leaves gradually bifurcate as they grow, the only version of its kind in the world. Asking himself in the poem:

*Is it truly a living being*
*That divides itself within itself?*

Goethe would conclude with the words:

*Do you not feel in my songs*
*That I am both one and doubled?*

He wrote out the poem in elegant cursive script and attached two Ginkgo leaves to the page, leaving it behind for Marianne as a sign of his love for her.

In the years that followed, Marianne and Goethe would carry on a letter exchange in which they continued to write each other poems based on the work of Hafez. It was out of this epistolary and poetic correspondence that *The West-East Divan* gradually grew, and we now know that portions of the volume were written by Marianne herself. Their letters to one another express an extraordinary depth of feeling, both for one another and for the poems of Hafez. It is fair to say that not since Schiller had Goethe found another soul who could propel his writing like Marianne von Willemer. She would one day give him a walking stick with a hoopoe bird engraved on it, a bird that symbolised communication and travel. Goethe kept the walking stick by his desk for the rest of his life.

On 6th June 1816, one summer after exchanging poems with Marianne von Willemer, Goethe's wife passed away. As he noted in his diary on that day, 'The pending end of my wife. The last fearful battle of her nature. She departed around midday. Emptiness and deathly silence in and around me. The ornate arrival of the Princess Ida. [Visits from] Meyer, Riemer. In the evening a brilliant illumination of the city. At midnight my wife is taken to the morgue. I lay the entire day in bed.' Goethe would write a poem commemorating the day, but two days later he would not attend her funeral.

One year later, Goethe's son, August, would marry Ottilie von Pogwisch, and together they would live in his father's home. Goethe was delighted to have a woman around the house again, especially one as attractive and precocious as Ottilie. A year later a grandson was born, Walther Wolfgang von Goethe, followed by two more grandchildren, Wolfgang Maximilian and Alma Cornelia, named after Goethe's sister. Upon the birth of Walther Wolfgang, Goethe named him an honorary junior member of the Mineralogical Society of Jena and presented him with a collection of stones in his cradle. Ever the admirer of little children ('children are the best educators,' he said), Goethe saw his grandchildren almost every day and would read the increasingly popular genre of children's illustrated books with them in the evenings. With their 'Apapa' they would look at maps of the Middle East and Goethe would give them presents like cameos of Trajan's Column in Rome. They loved to tell each other stories and Goethe records a time when Walther recounted for him the tale of the Magic Flute made famous by Mozart's opera. Goethe would go on numerous walks over the years with his grandchildren's mother, Ottilie, and she was one of the few privileged ones who heard Goethe read aloud from the second part of *Faust*. Even after August's death, Ottilie would stay with Goethe until he died.

Unfortunately, Ottilie and August's marriage was not a happy one. August was a melancholy man, a fate not uncommon for the children of great writers. He drank too much and there were numerous affairs on both sides. Ottilie was extremely social, and promiscuous, indulging in the literary socialising that her father-in-law's reputation made possible. She founded a multi-lingual journal called *Chaos* that seemed aptly to name the state of domestic discord in which they all lived. Eventually August was sent to Rome, like his father before him, but he would never return. He died of a fever in 1830 at the age of forty, outlived by his Olympian father. Upon learning of the death of his only son, Goethe was said to have made the rather shockingly caustic remark, 'I knew I created a mortal.' Not one of Goethe's grand-children left any descendants and at the death of Walther, the last surviving member of the Goethe family, all of Goethe's belongings and papers were bequeathed to the state of Sachsen-Weimar-Eisenach in 1885.

As the story of the Goethe family came to its gloomy end, Goethe's own personal fame was ensured for posterity through the public securement of his works. The Duchess Sophie von Sachsen-Weimar-Eisenach quickly assembled a team of six editors and over seventy assistants to begin producing a new critical edition of the great writer's works. Thirty-two years and 143 volumes later, the project would reach its conclusion in the famed 'Weimar Edition'. Like the tale of Saturn, the sacrifice of Goethe's offspring seemed to be the necessary precursor to his own spiritual survival.

# The Heavenly Archive

By the beginning of the 1820s, Goethe, who was now in his seventies, increasingly limited his travel to the environs of Weimar, although he still maintained his summer routine of visiting the spa town of Marienbad. It was here, in the summer of 1821, when he would meet the seventeen-year-old Ulrike von Levetzow, the last love of his life. The following summer Ulrike would be Goethe's constant companion. Dressed in her favourite tartan skirts in the mode of Sir Walter Scott, she would sit by the old man perched on the terrace during parties at the Brösigke's family estate. The next summer the seventy-two year-old Goethe asked his life-long confidant, the Duke Carl August, to ask her hand in marriage for him. The family politely declined. The result was Goethe's poem, *Marienbad Elegy*, which opened with the famous citation from his play, *Torquato Tasso*:

> *And if man falls silent in his pain,*
> *A god it was who allowed me to say what I have suffered.*

Besides the adolescent rejuvenation that the Marienbad episodes provided, Goethe's life in old age became increasingly routine. It was a life immersed in books, his own and those of others. A sample from his diaries from 8th December 1820 reads:

Letter to Frommann, 7th sheet of *Art and Antiquity* revised and the manuscript of *Wilhelm Meister's Travels*, sheets 2–47. Sketched letter to Dr Sulpiz Boisserée. Reading Wolf's *Prolegomena ad Homerum*. At midday a promenade with my daughter [Ottilie]. Three of us for lunch. Organised stone collection. Wolf's *Prolegomena*. Evening by myself, read through the next shipment of *Wilhelm Meister's Travels*. Then began the third volume of my autobiography, *From my Life*.

Goethe's life in the 1820s was defined by corresponding with publishers, editing his works that were in press, beginning new works or revising unfinished ones, bringing his papers and his collections in order, and avidly reading books sent to him by colleagues or recommended by the leading journals of the day.

Goethe's reading during this last decade became ever more international: the novels of Walter Scott and James Fenimore Cooper, the plays of Calderon, the work of Alessandro Manzoni, Serbian ballads translated by Therese von Jakob, and the poetry of Victor Hugo and Lord Byron. Of all his contemporaries, Goethe was most drawn to Byron. 'Only Byron can compete with me,' he once remarked. He began to read the French periodical, *Le Globe*, every day, excerpts from which he would publish in his journal, *Art and Antiquity*. It was a decade shaped by Goethe's growing interest in what the editors at *Le Globe* called '*le commerce intellectuel*', the circulations of cultural products that contributed to an increasingly global sensibility. As Goethe remarked to Eckermann, 'National literature has little to recommend it now. The epoch of world literature has arrived and everyone must now work to accelerate it.'

Goethe would carry on a long and quite touching correspondence during this period with his Scottish translator, Thomas Carlyle. In addition to their frequent exchanges of gifts, trinkets, books, and occasional poems, their letters are filled with thoughtful reflections on the nature of translation and its significance for cultural exchange. As Goethe remarked in one letter, 'Whatever one may say about the inadequacies of translation, it remains one of the most important and honourable occupations in the whole world.' In keeping with this globalis-ing spirit of his age, Goethe would eventually interest himself in Chinese literature, rewriting or 'translating' a series of poems dedicated to illustrious Chinese women which he had read in an English translation.

If Goethe became increasingly interested in the world, so too did the world in him. Weimar became its own kind of literary Mecca, receiving a steady stream of visitors from across Europe and the Atlantic. Ottilie was charged with the duties of coordinating the numerous admirers who sought an audience with the great writer. Mornings between eleven and twelve were reserved for individual visits by close friends. The elect were allowed to stay for lunch. Afternoon tea was for artistic gatherings or informal salons where Goethe would stay for as long as he felt interested or had the strength. The same was true for evening soirées. The universal language was French, except for Italians with whom Goethe loved to speak their native tongue.

The great poet Adam Mickiewicz came from Poland; George Ticknor, the American professor of Romance languages, came from Harvard; the soon-to-be famous English novelist William Thackeray from across the channel. 'Jupiter' was the epithet most often used by visitors to describe Goethe, and seldom did they not remark on the quaintness of Weimar and the intense backbiting of the local elite. Henry Crabb Robinson said that talking to Goethe was like talking to Shakespeare, Plato, Raphael and Socrates all at once. And for Augustus Bozzi Granville, a travelling physician, it was 'one of the highest gratifications which a traveller can enjoy, seeing and conversing with a genius whose fame, for the last fifty years, had filled all civilised Europe.'

The routines of this last decade were not without their unsettling moments. On 18th February 1823, Goethe suffered a heart attack. He survived, but his convalescence was slow and uncertain. After that summer's visit to Marienbad and its failed amorous end, for the next five years Goethe never left Weimar. Instead, he concentrated on organising all of his papers, began thinking about a new and final authorised edition of his collected works and made preparations for the oversight of his writing after his death. In June 1823, Goethe agreed to meet Johann Peter Eckermann, a young man interested in literature who had just completed a manuscript entitled *Essays on Poetry with Particular Reference to Goethe*. After a trial run, Goethe hired him as his secretary. From this relationship emerged one of the most famous works in German literary history, *Conversations with Goethe*, a vast compendium of Goethe's sayings from over almost a decade. Nietzsche claimed that it was the best book ever written in German.

Along with Eckermann, Goethe assembled a team of assistants to oversee his personal archive and the compilation of his final collected edition, which would eventually run to fifty-five volumes. These included the copyist Johann John, Friedrich Kräuter, secretary to the library, Johann Schuchardt, Karl Wilhelm Göttling, a professor of classical philology in Jena, and Friedrich Wilhelm Riemer who was the head librarian in Weimar. Even after Goethe's death, these men would be responsible for continuing to publish portions of Goethe's collected edition. As Goethe would one day say to a friend, 'My oeuvre is that of a collective being that bears the name Goethe.'

Goethe would one day endow the archive with a human shape in the fictional character of Makaria, a mysterious figure from his last novel who can see the entire universe in precise detail within her mind. Her role in the novel was to be an archivist and a network relay, preserving all of the writing she came in contact with and then circulating it among her ever-enlargening circle of friends. She captured for Goethe a theory of the 'supplemental self' that he developed in old age, a notion of the writer as a repository and a portal for every idea that human history had ever created. The poet mattered only in so far as he was continually supplemented by the world around him, as he incorporated this world into himself and then sent it back out for circulation. According to the aged Goethe, the poet was no longer the message, but the medium.

In 1824, Goethe approached his publisher, Johann Cotta, about producing a new collected edition. Negotiations were protracted – Goethe was notoriously difficult with his publishers – but eventually both parties agreed. Goethe was awarded the unprecedented sum of 100,000 Thaler. In addition he continued publishing his three major periodical projects, *On Art and Antiquity* and the two scientific serials, *On Morphology* and *On Natural Science*. He furthered his efforts at memorialising his life through the continuation of the autobiography, *From my Life*, with a piece on his adventures in France during the Napoleonic wars, as well as through an edition of his letter correspondence with Schiller. His preferred mode of composition these days was dictation. As his secretary Johann Christian Schuchardt described Goethe's method: 'With his hands extended and his body leaning to one side or the other he would bring the matter into balance and artful shape. Once done, he would customarily exclaim, "So right! Completely right!"' In this way, Goethe now began preparing everything for the collected edition and returned to two of his major works that remained incomplete: *Wilhelm Meister's Travels* and *Faust: Part II*.

The second half of *Faust* begins with the hero lying 'exhausted' in a flowery field after Gretchen's execution from Part I. He is surrounded by a chorus of spirits playing their Aeolian harps and singing of the blossoms of spring's rain. Faust awakens with the words, 'Life's pulse strikes with fresh vitality.' Nature has called him forth once more and it is the 'pulse' – the organic figure of recurrence, harmony, and eternal return – that captures man's ability to go on. He turns toward the sun and is blinded for a moment and declares in some of the most famous lines Goethe ever wrote,

> *Behind me, therfore, let the sun be glowing!*
> *The cataract, between the crags deep-riven,*
> *I thus behold  with rapture ever-growing.*
> *From plunge to plunge in thousand streams 't is given,*
> *And yet a thousand, to the valleys shaded,*
> *While foam and spray in air are whirled and driven.*
> *Yet how superb, across the tumult braided,*
> *The painted rainbow's changeful life is bending,*
> *Now clearly drawn, dissolving now and faded,*
> *And evermore the showers of dew descending!*
> *Of human striving there's no symbol fuller:*
> *Consider, and 't is easy comprehending –*
> *Life is there in the refracted color.*

The waterfall became the perfect symbol for Goethe's theory of human life. Those thousands of 'falls' mirrored the accidents and sins of mankind, out of which rose up something beautiful, something fleeting: the evanescent rainbow composed of thousands of tiny particles of mist that coalesced into a graceful form that intermittently shined back at us. The rainbow of the waterfall contained everything that mattered to Goethe: chance, spontaneity, refraction, diversity, form, fallibility and beauty.

On Faust would go for another 7,384 lines, careening through the world with Mephisto by his side. He will eventually meet Helen of Troy who will gradually morph into a medieval Germanic woman, linking the classical past with Germany's future. But at a cost. As they embrace, she disappears and all that is left of Western literature's most famous female character is her veil. On Faust goes. Nymphs, sphinxes, homunculi, kings, sirens, Philemon and Baucis, they're all there. Deep into Faust's old age, 'Care', in the sense of one's own worry or disquiet, will overtake him. Care will be what blinds Faust. 'Man is blind for his whole life,' Care says, 'Now, Faust, you are too in the end.' In response, Faust decides to become the archetype of the modern engineer in order to control nature and exploit it. His final act will be the construction of a massive irrigation project that turns out to be his grave. There is no surer critique of scientific progress than this.

But he will be saved in heaven, much to every secularist's surprise. How was it possible that after seducing and impregnating a young woman who murdered her mother and child and was executed in return; how after pillaging the natural world and ceaselessly striving only after his own pleasure; how after all this was it still possible to go to heaven? For Goethe it made perfect sense. Striving was everything, striving was thinking the good but never fulfilling it. It united idealism with our reality. Thus care and disquiet became the permanent states of modern man.

After ascending through various levels of heaven, Faust will see Gretchen transformed into the Una Poenitentium, the single penitent, followed by the Mater Gloriosa, as the famous last words of the tragedy are spoken by the Chorus Mysticus:

*The Eternal-Feminine*
*Lures us up and on.*

Das Ewig-Weibliche
Zieht uns hinan.

But on where? Even heaven for Goethe lacked a definitive ending.

# Goethe without End

On his eighty-second birthday, which would turn out to be his last, Goethe walked up to the cabin on top of the Kickelhahn, where he had once inscribed his poem, 'Above all peaks, there lies repose'. He had written the poem on the cabins' upstairs walls when he was thirty-one; it ended with the words:

*Only wait, soon*
*You too will rest.*

Goethe ascended the stairs to the upper floor, and upon seeing that his inscription was still there, we are told by his companion that tears began to roll down Goethe's cheeks as he quietly remarked to himself, 'Yes, soon you too will rest.'

Just a few weeks earlier Goethe had concluded his work on *Faust*, noting in his diary on 22nd July 1831, 'My main work achieved. Final dictation. The fair copy bound together.' The closing years of Goethe's life were marked by a remarkable degree of closure. *Faust* was 'finished', so too the *Wilhelm Meister* novel, which Goethe had once referred to as 'the problem of my life', and he was able to produce a new bilingual edition of *On the Metamorphosis of Plants*, which contained new ideas about what he called the 'spiral tendency' of all organic life. Forty volumes of the edition with Cotta were making their way through the press.

If these final years were characterised by an unusual element of completion that had never been a hallmark of Goethe's creativity, they were also marked by a growing sense of alienation from the world. He continued to outlive friends and family, as first his lifelong confidant and sovereign, the Duke Carl August, passed away in 1828, and then two years later his son died while in Rome. Goethe characteristically went on a short voyage in order to miss the funeral of Carl August (his son was buried in far-off Rome). Looking at the world around him, Goethe observed that it struck him as a 'velociferian age', a clever neologism that combined the idea of 'velocity' with that of 'luciferian'. Even in sleepy Weimar, everything and everyone appeared to be busy, moving fast and vastly productive. The coming Industrial Revolution was well underway, and Goethe read with both fascination and scepticism about great new projects like the Erie Canal in North America from the Duke's son who had travelled extensively across the continent. As we recall, Faust's own channel project would eventually turn out to be his grave.

When asked why he would not share *Faust* with his contemporaries – why he did not bother to publish it with the rest of his works in Cotta's edition – Goethe responded with the harsh judgment that 'our age is truly so absurd and confused that I have convinced myself that my hard-fought, long persecuted efforts for this curious creation would be poorly rewarded, ultimately driven aground, and, like a shipwreck, lie there covered over by the sands of time.' In the summer of 1830, Goethe would avidly follow the fall of the Bourbons in France and the institution of a constitutional monarchy after three revolutionary days in July. The world kept changing around him, always forwards and backwards.

In the years to come Goethe's reputation both soared and fell. He was the grandfather of European arts and letters, the last universal man who saw his poetry set to music by one of the greatest composers of the age, Franz Schubert, and his *Faust* turned into an opera by the one of the most popular, Hector

Berlioz. The renowned French painter Eugène Delacroix provided illustrations to a new French translation of *Faust*, part of a wave of *Faust* illustrations in the nineteenth century that surpassed 1,500 in all. Eckermann's *Conversations with Goethe* gave birth to a new genre of the authorial interview (pioneered by Boswell in his biography of Samuel Johnson), as a wave of 'Conversations with Goethe' were published in the years immediately following his death. Goethe had become an idol, a monument, a name that was capable of eliciting enormous emotional responses in his readers.

Yet despite the fame, Goethe was, as always, never fully in step with his age. Or you could say his age had passed him by. The luxury edition of his collected works with Cotta had trouble selling. A growing circle of detractors, what the novelist J.D. Salinger would have called the 'tearer-downers', had begun to form. As Wolfgang Menzel, the leader of the pack, wrote, Goethe offered Germans 'a fantastical Egoism with the pleasures of superficiality and self-divination at the expense of religion, fatherland and honour. He made us like the effete Narcissus reflecting ourselves in the spring while behind our backs they were readying their knives and chains.' Goethe's relentless pursuit of himself had no place in a world that demanded sacrifice for political ends.

The first statue erected in the German territories in honour of a poet, constructed in 1837, was of not Goethe, but Friedrich Schiller. The hundredth anniversary of Goethe's birth passed without notice, but ten years later in 1859, Schiller's birth was celebrated like that of no other German hero ever before. The spiritual life of Europe after the Congress of Vienna, despite the repression, or perhaps because of it, was increasingly driven by politics and nationalism. Journalism was the new *leitmedium* and *littérature engagée* the code word of the day. The poem set most often to music in the nineteenth century was not by Goethe, but by the lawyer Nikolaus Becker who sung of the 'free German Rhine'. The literary movement of 'Young Germany' was under way, and its aim was to overturn the reactionary political programme set in place by Metternich. Its idols were Hegel and Saint-Simon and its apex (and end) was the year 1848, which saw the publication of Friedrich Engels' and Karl Marx's *Communist Manifesto* in London and the failed 'March Revolution' for national unity in the German states.

Goethe's seeming incompatibility with the urgent questions of modern life would change forever on Sunday 28th June 1896, when a ceremony was held to mark the completion of a new building in Weimar: the Goethe and Schiller Archive. It was a day of extreme optimism; reverent speeches were delivered, Beethoven's Ninth Symphony was played, and newspapers made grand pronouncements, comparing the archive to the Library of Alexandria, calling Weimar the Athens on the Ilm, and anointing the new structure a 'fortress of the spirit', 'temple', and 'citadel'. Even *The Chicago Times Herald* reported the story, remarking, 'The whole may well be named the Pantheon of German Literature – the most unique and valuable in the whole history of literature.' Standing imperiously on a hill overlooking, indeed dwarfing, the small town below it, the imposing structure was a vivid sign of the assured permanence of Goethe's afterlife.

Goethe would become, to take but one example, a key reference for the establishment of the brief German experiment with democracy between the First and Second World Wars known as the 'Weimar Republic'. He would again be a key figure enlisted by the Nazis, who sent pocket editions of *Faust* to the soldiers at the front. Goethe was an icon too for those Germans who emigrated during the war, both internally and externally, and dreamt of a more humane German past and future. Thomas Mann, in exile in southern California while his homeland collapsed, chose to title his final novel *Doctor Faustus*. And during the coming Cold War, Goethe would be a key battlefront between East and West Germany. Today, there are thirty-four Goethe societies worldwide and 147 Goethe Institutes in eighty-three countries. The most recent completed bibliography of books and essays on Goethe – which ends in 1990 – contains 20,621 entries. Goethe, like Shakespeare, is now a global industry. Or as Nietzsche quipped in one of his many aphorisms, 'Goethe, not just a good and great man, but a culture.'

Through all of the uses and abuses of Goethe's legacy, there still remains the question of what Goethe's actual life and work meant. Never before have we known so much about any one writer. And never since has someone remained so elusive and enigmatic. It is precisely this fugitive quality of Goethe's life, I suspect, that invites us to fill in perpetually what he means. Goethe was a chemist, botanist, anatomist, physicist, Privy Counsellor, essayist, editor, theatre director, novelist, and poet. And he was none of these. He was a political reactionary who was one of the most experimental writers in history. He came to embody the spirit of his age – indeed it became *his* age – and yet he was the most protean of characters, not to mention one of the most aloof. He never stayed the same and his writing never did either. 'What!' he once cried, 'have I reached the age of eighty merely to think the same things all the time?' His ultimate aim, he said, was to enjoy life with the enjoyers. *Mit Genießern zu genießen.*

If Goethe's work is so difficult for us to access today it is because it is so thoroughly stamped with an uncompromising individual vision. As much as he has come to be regarded as the last Renaissance Man, there was in the end never any unity to all of his parts, just an unceasing spontaneity, creativity, and curiosity. He was always haunted by the sense of what he called his 'false tendencies', to go off on a tangent that was in fact a dead end. But they were only 'false' because in the coming age of specialisation and progress – in the Age of the *Résumé* – there was no more room for the eclecticism of human nature. Goethe will forever stand as the sign of the irreducible polyphony of our character, a reminder of the fundamental miscellaneity of the human self.

On the morning of 16th March 1832, Goethe's physician, Dr Carl Vogel, came to visit him earlier than usual. Goethe complained of a fever and chest pains since taking a walk the night before. The doctor diagnosed Goethe with a severe catarrhal fever. Goethe was given a solution of ammonium chloride, Epsom salt, and barley paste. By that evening he was feeling somewhat better, and his usual liveliness and humour had returned. Goethe's condition improved until the night of the nineteenth, when he began to feel a powerful chill in his limbs and extraordinary pain in his chest. The doctor arrived the next morning and saw that Goethe's face had become strained and anxious and had lost its colour. His eyes appeared deeply sunken in his face. Valerian ether was administered and he was given a mixture of anise oil and ammonia taken alternately with peppermint and camomile tea. His condition stabilised and he slept well the next night. The doctor reported that Goethe was very calm throughout. By the following evening, the rattling in Goethe's chest had returned, his fingers were ice-cold. He gradually lost his ability to speak. His condition worsened until the following day. As Dr Vogel reported in his notes on 22nd March 1832, 'At eleven thirty the dying man comfortably positioned himself in the left corner of his armchair, and a good deal of time passed before those of us around him had realised that Goethe had passed away. Such a gentle death completed the good fortune of this richly gifted being.'

# Biographical note

Andrew Piper is an Assistant Professor in the Department of German studies and an Associate member of the Department of Art History and Communication Studies at McGill University in Canada. He is the author of *Dreaming in Books: The Making of the Bibliographic Imagination in the Romantic Age* (Chicago 2009) and two translations by Goethe, both with Hesperus: *The Man of Fifty* and *The Madwoman on a Pilgrimage*. He is currently at work on a project on Goethe, print and autobiography entitled, *The Medium of Myself.*

# Acknowledgement

The long quotation from Faust on pages 83, 84 and 106 are taken from *Faust: A Tragedy*, translated by Bayard Taylor (1884).

## SELECTED TITLES FROM HESPERUS PRESS

### Brief Lives

| Author | Title |
| --- | --- |
| Andrew Brown | *Brief Lives: Gustave Flaubert* |
| Andrew Brown | *Brief Lives: Stendhal* |
| David Carter | *Brief Lives: Marquis de Sade* |
| Robert Chandler | *Brief Lives: Alexander Pushkin* |
| Anthony Cummins | *Brief Lives: Emile Zola* |

### Classics, Modern Voices and New Fiction

| Author | Title | Foreword writer |
| --- | --- | --- |
| M. Ageyev | *A Romance with Cocaine* | Toby Young |
| Charles Baudelaire | *On Wine and Hashish* | Margaret Drabble |
| Anton Chekhov | *The Exclamation Mark* | Lynne Truss |
| Joseph Conrad | *The Tale* | Philip Hensher |
| Fyodor Dostoevsky | *The Eternal Husband* | Andrew Miller |
| J. von Eichendorff | *Life of a Good-for-nothing* | |
| Laurent Gaudé | *The Scortas' Sun* | |
| Yasmine Ghata | *The Calligraphers' Night* | |
| Johann Wolfgang von Goethe | *The Madwoman on a Pilgrimage* | Lewis Crofts |
| Johann Wolfgang von Goethe | *The Man of Fifty* | A.S. Byatt |
| E.T.A. Hoffmann | *Mademoiselle Scudéri* | Gilbert Adair |
| Joris-Karl Huysmans | *With the Flow* | Simon Callow |
| Franz Kafka | *Metamorphosis* | Martin Jarvis |
| Klaus Mann | *Alexander* | Jean Cocteau |
| Prosper Mérimée | *Carmen* | Philip Pullman |
| Alexander Pushkin | *The Tales of Belkin* | Adam Thirlwell |
| Leo Tolstoy | *The Forged Coupon* | Andrew Miller |
| Heinrich von Kleist | *The Marquise of O-* | Andrew Miller |
| Emile Zola | *The Flood* | |